WRITE THROUGH CHICAGO

WRITE THROUGH
CHICAGO

40 CREATIVE WRITING PROMPTS FOR DEVELOPING WRITERS
ALIGNS TO NCTE & COMMON CORE STATE STANDARDS

LEARN ABOUT A CITY BY WRITING ABOUT A CITY

Mark Henry Larson & Bob Boone

To Jay Amberg, our friend

BOOKS BY MARK HENRY
LARSON & BOB BOONE

Write Through Chicago
Amika Press

Joan's Junk Shop
Good Year Books

Moe's Cafe
Good Year Books

BOOKS BY MARK HENRY
LARSON

The Creative Writing Handbook
Good Year Books

BOOKS BY BOB BOONE

Forest High
Amika Press

Inside Job: A Life of Teaching
Puddin'head Press

Developing Your Test-Taking Skills
National Textbook Company

Language and Literature
Ed., McDougal Littell, Inc

*Verbal Review and Workbook
for the SAT*
Harcourt Brace Jovanovich
Publishers

Hack
Follett Publishing Company

Using Media
Peacock Press

First Edition   ISBN 13: 978-1-937484-15-6
AMIKA PRESS   466 Central Ave #23 Northfield IL 60093   847 920 8084
info@amikapress.com   Available for purchase on amikapress.com
Edited by John Manos and Ann Wambach. Cover photograph by Robert Williams. Author photographs
by Deborah Larson and Sue Boone. Designed & typeset by Sarah Koz. Body in Ehrhardt, designed by
Nicholas Kis in late 1600s, digitized by Monotype in 1991. Titles in Balboa Light and Condensed, designed by Jim Parkinson in 2001. Thanks to Nathan Matteson.

CONTENTS

The Headlines

INTRODUCTION TO THE STUDENT

A writing book and a history book? Sounds like a bit of a stretch. How good can that be?

Well…we think it can be *very* good.

This is a writing book because, relying on your memory and imagination, you will explore with your own words an array of subjects. You'll craft stories, poems, arguments, monologues, diaries, letters, and various other forms of writing. At times, you'll write in your voice, at times, in someone else's. Sometimes you will direct your words to people like yourself and sometimes to people utterly unlike you. And the inspiration for all of this writing will be Chicago history—the big events like the Great Fire, the minor events like the Beatles coming to town, individuals like Jane Addams, places like the White City, and dramatic events like the Pullman Strike.

Each of the 40 sections of the book starts off with a *Headline.* The headline announces something significant in our city's history—an achievement, a celebration, a tragedy, a new trend starting, an old trend ending. The headline may concern something political like an election, something cultural, or something commercial.

After checking out the headline, you'll read a short *Background* section. This will tell you enough about the subject of the headline to make you familiar with it, but only enough to get started—the skeleton, but not the flesh.

This will be followed by *Remember.* Here you'll connect what you already know to what's in the headline. For this you might write a personal narrative or essay or a description. And these words will flow from your experience and link with the subject of the headline.

In *Discover,* you'll expand what you know. You'll find subjects and questions and suggestions on where to go for the answers to the questions posed. This might be a website, a newspaper article, a book, or an actual place like a museum or cultural center. You'll shape what you've learned into essays that explain what you now understand. Or, you might write a rap or make a poster or show off your new knowledge in other ways.

Many of the Discover questions can be completed in a short time. Others require more planning and execution and additional equipment such as PowerPoint software or a poster board. These longer ones might provide you with an idea for a history fair such as the Chicago Metro History Fair. But even if you do not actually create a PowerPoint presentation, you should consider the steps involved. These more ambitious assignments will give you a further notion of the connections that can be made in this book.

In the next section, *Decide,* you'll construct an argument. You might take a position on the significance of the event itself or you might argue about the relevance of one of the related aspects. Again, some of the longer, more demanding assignments might be good candidates for a Chicago history fair.

In the *Imagine* section you will create something new—a story, a short play, a monologue—that will add more meaning to what you've been studying. You might become one of the characters in the event. You might place the event in a modern setting. You might write about it from a new point of view.

By the end of all of this, you will know the names of important places in Chicago and why they are important. You will understand issues and trends. You'll appreciate the builders of the city. You'll have a sense of why Chicago resembles other cities and how it is utterly unique. You will better understand where its reputation comes from and to what degree it deserves that reputation.

If nothing else, you'll have a better idea than most people of what it was like to be alive at certain moments: to be at Lincoln's Chicago Funeral, at the opening of the Columbian Exposition, in the crowd at the Haymarket Riot, driving to Riverview Amusement Park, chomping down on the first McDonald's burger, or to be in the crowd at Grant Park to watch Barack Obama deliver his presidential acceptance speech.

Along the way you will also start to realize just how much more there is to learn about this remarkable city and be motivated to get out there and keep learning.

So, is this a silly idea? Not really. Not if you're someone curious about Chicago and anxious to write.

WRITE THROUGH AMERICA WEBSITE

A unique feature offered by *Write Through Chicago* is its accompanying web-site: **writethroughamerica.com**. This website provides both teachers and students with an array of writing support options:

Headlines

The site includes hundreds of suggested links to primary and secondary sources, each specifically itemized to correspond to the 240 research prompts assigned in the 40 chapters of *Write Through Chicago*. This list is continuously reviewed and updated as certain links turn inactive and others become available.

Student Writing

Students have the opportunity to submit their own writing for publication on the website. Teachers and students can access these student writing samples based on *Write Through Chicago* prompts and read annotated comments by *Write Through Chicago*'s authors. Student submissions also become eligible for writing contests sponsored by Write Through America.

Core Standards

An itemized set of Core Standards charts indicates which Writing, Speaking and Listening, Reading Literature/Reading for Information, and Language standards are met by individual *Write Through Chicago* units.

TO THE CLASSROOM TEACHER

As a teacher you have probably often thought, "Sure, I'd like to try that, but I've got way too much on my plate as it is." As a teacher you have always been busy; but now with the current shift to mandated alignment to Common Core Standards, you are busier still. So, although it is intriguing to have a new set of interesting activities to use in your classroom, they may be of limited use if they do not fit within the constraints of your curriculum.

The good news is that *Write Through Chicago* is designed to meet the dual requirements of what you *want* to teach as well as what you may *have* to teach. In the course of providing what we believe is a unique approach for students to "learn about a city by writing about a city," *Write Through Chicago* also provides the classroom teacher with 320 writing activities, each aligning to the Common Core Standards for Writing, Speaking and Listening, Reading Literature/Reading for Information, and Language.

Common Core Standards

The Common Core Standards for Writing consist of three types of writing: Argument, Exposition, and Narrative (both personal and fictional). Each one of the 40 chapters of *Write Through Chicago* covers all 11 Common Core Standards for Writing:

1 Text Type and Purpose: Argument
Each Decide section consists of two persuasive essay prompts.

2 Text Type and Purpose: Exposition
Each Discover section consists of a variety of expository research projects (see standards 7–9).

3 Text Type and Purpose: Narrative
Several Remember prompts are personal narrative assignments; many Imagine prompts are fictional narrative assignments. The remaining assignments in these sections redirect the narrative approach into alternative formats such as letters, diary entries, dramatic scenes, etc.

4 Production and Distribution: Clarity and Coherence
Each of the 40 units includes eight writing projects; all 320 stress clarity and coherence in writing.

5 Production and Distribution: Planning, Revising, and Rewriting
Each of the 40 units includes eight writing projects; all 320 require planning, revising, and rewriting.

6 Production and Distribution: Technology

The **writethroughamerica.com** support website provides updated links to online sites for obtaining information for each of the 240 prompts in the Discover and Decide sections.

7 Research: Research Projects

Each Discover section has four short-term research assignments; each Decide section includes two long-range research assignments.

8 Research: Multiple Print and Digital Sources

Each assignment in the Discovery and Decide sections requires students to use a variety of media sources, including online sites, books, films, etc.

9 Research: Literary and Informational Texts

The Decide section requires students to analyze information obtained from various perspectives and to synthesize the findings into a persuasive, collaborated argument.

10 Range of Writing: Single Sitting

The personal narrative prompts in the Remember sections are designed to be completed in a single sitting as are the written elements of the Discover research prompts.

11 Range or Writing: Extended Writing

The fictional story prompt in each Imagine section and the two persuasive argument assignments in each Decide section require an extended writing approach.

As for the remaining three categories of Core Standards, the 40 *Write Through Chicago* chapters collectively meet all of the standards for "Speaking and Listening" and "Reading for Literature/Reading for Information," as well as most of those for "Language." To access itemized charts breaking down how these standards are met by individual chapters of *Write Through Chicago*, visit our support website: **writethroughamerica.com**.

Standardized Testing

Along with being required to align their assignments to the Common Core Standards for Writing, many teachers must also allocate class time to prepare students for standardized testing such as the ACT. Although *Write Through Chicago* is not designed as an ACT preparation book per se, the reading required to complete the chapters' research and writing activities provides reading experience in the four subject areas covered on the ACT Reading Comprehension Test: Literature, Social Studies, Humanities, and Natural Science. The 40 headline events in *Write Through Chicago* draw from these same four categories, and each is marked with an appropriate icon for easy identification.

Bloom's Taxonomy

Furthermore, for those teachers interested in incorporating Benjamin Bloom's Taxonomy of Learning Objectives in the classroom, the writing assignments in *Write Through Chicago* work as well:

A Lower Level Thinking (Knowledge, Comprehension, and Application)
Each Background section ends with a prompt requiring students to conduct some background research on the Chicago event and then write a concise summary of the information obtained. This activity requires the student to know what type of event is being studied (knowledge), understand the material presented (comprehension), and convey the pertinent material in concise form (application).

B Higher Level Thinking (Analysis, Synthesis, and Evaluation)
The personal narrative from the Remember section requires not only a comprehensive retention of the details of the memory itself, but also the ability to break down the whole (analysis) into a coherent and focused story. The Imagine section's fictional story prompt poses a "what if?" scenario (synthesis), requiring students to go beyond their familiar world of the present to the less familiar world of Chicago's past. The persuasive essay prompts of the Decide section provide an opportunity for students to take the material they have analyzed and synthesized and present a corroborated argument in which they take a stand (evaluation) on a debatable issue.

Writing Portfolios

Given the format of *Write Through Chicago,* teachers requiring their students to keep writing portfolios will find the book especially useful. For example, if a teacher assigns a personal narrative, a short story, a report, a multimedia speech project, a poem, a critique, and two argument essays to be submitted over the course of a term, students could select single chapters such as "Fire Rages Through Chicago" or "First McDonald's Franchise Opens" and find prompts along with appropriate research links for each of those activities. Other students, however, could choose to go through multiple chapters, selecting individual activities from each to complete and meet the requirements of the portfolio. With each chapter presenting eight different prompts and with the book offering 40 different types of writing activities overall, students should have little trouble finding something in *Write Through Chicago* to meet their needs and catch their interests.

And Finally...

Knowing that *Write Through Chicago* aligns to these various recognized standards leaves you free to concentrate on other matters, such as helping your students connect with the remarkable city of Chicago and its fascinating history. So whether you're a History of Chicago teacher looking for a supplementary text, a teacher offering Chicago history as an activity, an American History teacher looking for opportunities to share moments about one of America's most influential cities, or even a Creative Writing teacher looking for some fresh prompts, *Write Through Chicago* offers the means to help you and your students "learn about a city by writing about a city." Enjoy the trip!

Mark Henry Larson
& Bob Boone

THE HEADLINES

1772
JEAN-BAPTISTE POINTE DUSABLE MOVES IN

Jean-Baptiste Pointe DuSable. Depiction from *History of Chicago* (1884) by Alfred Theodore Andreas. Available from Wikimedia Commons file: Jean_Baptiste_Point_du Sable_Andreas_1884.jpg, accessed August 20, 2013.

Background

In the year 2010, the population of greater Chicago was more than nine million. In 1790, the permanent population of this area was four—Jean-Baptiste Pointe DuSable, his wife Catherine, and their two children. Missionaries and explorers had passed through, and Native Americans lived nearby, but this man, probably from Haiti, and his family were the only permanent residents. They lived near the mouth of the Chicago River.

Very little is known about DuSable and his wife, but records indicate that he was a trader and a farmer. He had a large house along with many smaller houses, a barn, and animals.

Check out the display devoted to Jean-Baptiste Pointe DuSable at the *Chicago: Crossroads of America* exhibit at the Chicago History Museum.

Search online at the Encyclopedia of Chicago on the Chicago History Museum's website to discover more photos, articles, and facts about this early pioneer.

Visit the website of the DuSable Museum of African American History.

Now write a concise summary on the life and accomplishments of Jean-Baptiste Pointe DuSable.

Remember

DuSable must have been a hardworking fellow: he lived off the land, started his own business, and labored long hours—all at the mercy of nature.

Who is one of the hardest working, most productive people that you know? Explain why you consider this person to be so hardworking. Here are some questions to get you started:

1 How do you know this person?   2 In what areas of his or her life is this person hardworking?   3 What is a good example of this person's impressive efforts?   4 What is another example?   5 How has this person's life been affected by these efforts?   6 How does this person relate to others?   7 What would be a perfect job for this person? 8 What would be a terrible job?   9 What might change this person's attitude toward work?   10 Who might this person's role model be?

Combine your answers into a profile of this remarkable individual.

Go Online

Go to **chicago.writethroughamerica.com/dusable** to access useful links and student writing samples for the Discover and Decide prompts.

Discover

A What was the life of a fur trader like? Learn more about the subject; then write a report entitled "A Day in the Life of a Fur Trader."

B Jean-Baptiste Pointe DuSable's wife Catherine was a member of the Potawatomi nation, Native Americans who inhabited much of the Great Lakes region. By 1840, however, the Potawtomi were gone from Illinois. Read about the culture of these people. Then create a timeline poster about their history to use as a visual aid for a speech.

C Jean-Baptiste Pointe DuSable, a black man, was Chicago's first permanent resident. One hundred and thirty years later, the Great Migration of more than a million African Americans from the rural South began. Many made their way to Chicago and settled in communities such as Bronzeville. Learn more about the rich history of Bronzeville. Then write a free verse poem or collection of haiku capturing the feel of this community.

D The commemorative marker devoted to Jean-Baptiste and Catherine DuSable at the corner of Kinzie and Pine Streets is just one of many such memorials dedicated to famous Chicagoans. Scattered throughout the city, these memorials form a rich and varied source of local history. Take a camera to a number of these sites and create a PowerPoint presentation on these tributes.

Decide

A In your opinion, what made DuSable's life especially difficult? Write an essay presenting the five biggest obstacles he faced.

B Write an essay arguing that the city founded by Jean-Baptiste Pointe DuSable turned out to be a wonderful place to live.

JEAN-BAPTISTE POINTE DUSABLE MOVES IN 5

Imagine

You decide to travel back in time to have a conversation with Jean-Baptiste Pointe DuSable. But before you actually meet him, you write him a letter telling him what downtown Chicago looks like today—more than 200 years later.

What are you going to tell him about...

1 First impressions. 2 Buildings. 3 Various groups of people.
4 Clothing. 5 Noises and smells. 6 Work and occupations.
7 Food. 8 Parks. 9 Entertainment. 10 Anything else he would find bewildering.

Shape these answers and any other pertinent information into a friendly letter to Jean-Baptiste Pointe DuSable. Remember that he has no idea what Chicago looks like today. When he looks out of the window of his house, he sees water and prairies and forest, and that is it.

AUGUST 15, 1812
GARRISON AMBUSHED!
FORT DEARBORN BURNED!

Detail from Fort Dearborn Massacre Monument. Carl Rohl-Smith (1912). Available from Wikimedia Commons file: Carl_Rohl-Smith_Fort_Dearborn_Massacre 1893.jpg, accessed August 20, 2013.

Background

By 1803 the area we call Chicago had added a few more families. The land, though not yet part of a state, was officially under the control of the United States government. That year the government decided to build a fort on the Chicago River. It was completed the next year, and a small settlement formed around it. A young man named John Kinzie was the head of the settlement.

In 1812 a war between the United States and Great Britain and its local Indian allies had broken out. The U.S. government thought it would be better for the small group of people living at Fort Dearborn to abandon the area. The group, made up of soldiers, women, and children, numbered 148.

They left on August 15, 1812, but they were attacked by 500 Potawatomi Indians, and 86 members of the group were killed. The commander of the fort and his wife were captured and ransomed. The next day the Indians burned the fort to the ground. It was rebuilt in 1816.

Check out the display devoted to Fort Dearborn at the *Chicago: Crossroads of America* exhibit at the Chicago History Museum.

Search online at the Encyclopedia of Chicago on the Chicago History Museum's website to discover more illustrations, articles, and facts about the conflict at Fort Dearborn.

Now that you have familiarized yourself with the subject, write a concise summary of the event.

Remember

For reasons that are not totally clear, the Indians resorted to violence, and the results were tragic. Violence, unfortunately, has been a big part of Chicago's history. What opinions have you formed about violence from…

1 The news? 2 Television and movies? 3 Books? 4 Video games?
5 Competitive sports? 6 Sports fans? 7 Ancient history?
8 Recent history? 9 Behavior of young children? 10 Behavior of students at your school?

Consider at least three of these sources, and then write a short, personal essay explaining your attitude. Write in the present tense. Do you consider violence inevitable? Desirable? Correctable? Would you ever resort to violence?

Go Online

Go to **chicago.writethroughamerica.com/dearborn** to access useful links and student writing samples for the Discover and Decide prompts.

Discover

A The flag of Chicago has four stars, each representing a significant event in Chicago history: Fort Dearborn, the Chicago Fire, the World's Columbian Exposition, and the Century of Progress Exposition. Examine a timeline of Chicago history; then select four alternative events to replace the original four.

B The events that transpired at Fort Dearborn took place in the larger context of the War of 1812 between the United States and Great Britain. Learn more about Great Britain's most powerful Shawnee ally, Tecumseh. Create a poster or PowerPoint presentation on Tecumseh and his connection to the fighting on the American frontier.

C Although by 1840 the Potawatomi had abandoned the Chicago area, descendants of more than 50 Native American cultures currently call Chicago home. Learn more about the Native American people living in Chicago by visiting the website of the American Indian Center of Chicago, and design a brochure for the center.

D On February 22, 2007, officials at the University of Illinois decided to discontinue using Chief Illiniwek as the official mascot of the university. Learn more about the reasons behind the university's decision. Interview classmates, family members, and friends to determine their perspectives on the Chief Illiniwek controversy. Write an article on what you have discovered, and submit it to your school or local newspaper.

Decide

A Examine the photo of Carl Rohl-Smith's memorial to the Fort Dearborn Massacre/Battle, *Black Partridge Saving Mrs. Helm*, at the top of this section. Although this statue was once a famous Chicago landmark, it now sits in storage in a warehouse. Research information on the incident it depicts and the controversy that surrounds the statue.

Given what you have discovered in your research, what would you consider to be an appropriate acknowledgement of the events of August 15, 1812? Design and justify a fitting memorial to the events at Fort Dearborn.

B In 1899 Simon Pokagon, a 19th-century Potawatomi writer whose father was present at the Battle of Fort Dearborn, declared, "When whites are killed, it is a massacre; when Indians are killed, it is a fight." Are the controversial events of August 15, 1812, best left forgotten, or is there something worthwhile to be learned from revisiting them? Further research the "battle" vs. "massacre" controversy, and write an essay arguing for or against the significance of this debate.

Imagine

You survive the Indian attack near Fort Dearborn and somehow make it to safety. Tell your story, making sure to include…

1 Who you are and why you were at Fort Dearborn. **2** Some friendly Indians. **3** Some not-so-friendly Indians. **4** Midwestern summer heat. **5** Hunger. **6** Flat terrain. **7** Lake Michigan. **8** Memories of the massacre. **9** Some incidents of good luck. **10** An encounter with a friendly trapper.

Write this in the present tense as a diary entry. Describe your feelings. Use your imagination to invent credible details.

1845
ABOLITIONISTS MEET AT TAILOR'S SHOP

John Jones. Portrait by Aaron E. Darling, *c.* 1865. Chicago History Museum. Image cropped and tinted.

Background

Antislavery activity had been going on for many years before the start of the Civil War. The abolitionist headquarters in Chicago was a tailor shop owned by John Jones, a free African American from North Carolina. Frederick Douglass and other abolitionists would meet at Jones's home. John Brown stopped there on his way to leading an armed uprising at Harpers Ferry, Virginia. The tailor shop and home were both stops on the Underground Railroad, a secret route of safe houses for aiding escaped slaves making their way to Canada.

Check out the exhibit devoted to the Underground Railroad at the DuSable Museum of African American History.

Search online at the Encyclopedia of Chicago on the Chicago History Museum's website to discover more photos, articles, and facts about the Underground Railroad.

Now write a concise summary of the life of social activist John Jones.

Remember

John Jones was many things: a black man, a businessman, a political activist, and, later, an elected Chicago official. But most of all, John Jones was a helper. No matter how busy he might be, he helped people get what they needed.

Describe a time in your life when you successfully helped someone.

1 How old were you? What was really important to you at that time?
2 How did you know the person you helped?   3 What was this person's problem?   4 What would have happened if the problem had not been solved?   5 Did the person ask for your help?   6 Did the person know you were going to help, or did you keep it a secret?   7 How did you start to help?   8 At any point did the task seem too hard? Explain.
9 How did you know you were successful?   10 How did this affect your relationship with the person?

Go Online

Go to **chicago.writethroughamerica.com/jjones** to access useful links and student writing samples for the Discover and Decide prompts.

Discover

A The lives of free African Americans in the days of slavery were far from ideal. Although they were not slaves, they still encountered racial prejudice and social injustice. Learn more about the subject, and make a list of 10 facts you discovered about the lives of free blacks in the pre-war North.

B Since it was illegal to teach slaves to read or write, most were illiterate. This made it even more difficult for those attempting to flee the South and make their way to Canada. Some historians believe that enslaved women may have passed on secret messages to escaping slaves by means of a secret code incorporated into the designs of their homemade quilts. Others dispute this notion. Research the topic and present the two views in a speech or Power-Point presentation.

C Although John Jones was a remarkable person, it can be argued that his wife, Mary Richardson Jones, was just as remarkable. Learn more about her life, then design a commemorative plaque honoring her.

D A number of underground railroad "stations" existed in what is now sub-urban DuPage County. One of those still standing is Graue Mill, situated on the banks of Salt Creek. Visit Graue Mill and some of the other stations. Take your camera and create a PowerPoint presentation on the sites.

Decide

A Some historians view John Jones's houseguest John Brown as a martyr for a just cause. Others consider him to be a terrorist. Learn more about this con-troversial figure. Then write an essay either defending or attacking his legacy.

B During the Civil War, John Jones raised a regiment of black troops who lat-er saw action in the front lines. Learn more about the 200,000 African Ameri-cans who fought in the Union army. Watch the 1989 film *Glory* (R), which tells the story of the 54th Massachusetts Volunteer Infantry, one of the first black units to serve in the Civil War. Then write an essay using this thesis starter: "The 1989 film *Glory* does/does not accurately portray the experi-ences of black soldiers in the Civil War by…"

Imagine

John Jones is looking for someone to help with his business and with his political affairs. You find out about the opportunity and decide you are uniquely qualified.

Before contacting John Jones, you need to answer these questions:

1 Why do you object to slavery on moral principles?   2 Why do you feel slavery goes against American values?   3 What damage does slavery do to society?   4 How do you feel about acts of violence to oppose slavery?   5 How do you feel about helping fugitive slaves?   6 What enemies will you make by working with Jones? Why are you not afraid? 7 How have you shown that you are a hard worker?   8 How have you shown that you are a skilled worker?   9 How have you shown that you can get along with intense people like John Brown?   10 How have you shown that you can keep up with smart people like Frederick Douglass?

Shape these responses into a letter to John Jones.

DECEMBER 31, 1855
CITY PULLS ITSELF OUT OF THE MUD

Raising of the Briggs House. Chicago Historical Society. Available from Wikimedia Commons file: Briggs_house.jpg, accessed August 20, 2013.

Background

By 1855 Chicago had been an official city for 18 years, and it was growing fast. Its location on the shore of Lake Michigan was a tremendous advantage, and this grew even greater with the digging of a canal connecting Lake Michigan to the Mississippi River.

But all this water meant mud and floods and disease. The people in government and the private landowners decided a solution would be to raise the city. This would make room for an adequate sewage system and create more dry land.

The plan worked. Engineers used elaborate systems of jacks to lift entire buildings an average of six feet, and by early 1862 Chicago was a much drier and cleaner place.

Read Donald L. Miller's *City of the Century: The Epic of Chicago and the Making of America* (pp. 124–131) to learn more about the raising of Chicago's streets.

Search online at the Encyclopedia of Chicago on the Chicago History Museum's website to discover more photos, articles, and facts about this ambitious project of raising the street grades.

Remember

Recall a time that you were involved in or witnessed a successful group building project. This effort may have taken place at school or elsewhere. It might have been a backyard snow fort, clubhouse, or even a lemonade stand. Although it was not on the scale of raising Chicago, in its own way it was important.

1 How old were you at the time? What mattered to you?   2 What problem was the project intended to solve?   3 How would the project solve the problem?   4 What was the overall plan?   5 Who was involved in the project?   6 What, if anything, was your role?   7 How did the project begin?   8 What unexpected problems occurred? 9 How was the project completed?   10 What was the overall success of the project?

Write this as a news story. Make sure the first paragraph answers the questions: who, what, when, where, why, and how.

Go Online

Go to **chicago.writethroughamerica.com/citypulls** to access useful links and student writing samples for the Discover and Decide prompts.

Discover

A In 1854 more than 1,400 Chicagoans died of cholera, a tragedy that served to motivate city planners to take on the massive endeavor to raise Chicago streets and improve sanitation. Write a one-page report on this disease, which still accounts for more than 100,000 deaths globally each year.

B The raising of Chicago's streets and the installation of a storm-sewer system eventually led to the decision in 1900 to reverse the flow of the Chicago River—so that it would flow away from Lake Michigan rather than into the lake—in order to prevent the contamination of the city's supply of water from the lake. Create a PowerPoint presentation on this truly remarkable river with its reversed flow—one of the greatest feats of modern engineering.

C *"It is hopeless for the occasional visitor to try to keep up with Chicago— she outgrows his prophecies faster than he can make them. She is always a novelty; for she is never the Chicago you saw when you passed through the last time."* *(Mark Twain)* Using your own drawings, online images, or clip art, create a children's book or graphic novel chapter that presents an illustrated story of the progress made in Chicago from its incorporation as a city in 1837 to the project of raising its streets begun in 1855 and completed in 1858.

D Take an actual or a virtual tour of the Chicago River, and write an article on the experience. Illustrate the article with photos you have taken yourself or have downloaded from the Internet.

Decide

A Imagine what a challenge it must have been to convince the Chicago City Council to approve a 20-year project to raise the level of Chicago's streets several feet. Using the first-person voice of a proponent of the plan, write a speech to the council arguing for the adoption of this plan.

B The influx of Asian carp in the Mississippi River basin is a cause of concern to ecologists who want to prevent this invasive species from entering Lake Michigan via the Chicago Sanitary and Ship Canal. One proposed solution to the problem would be to undo the reversal of the flow of the Chicago River. Research the Asian carp invasion and the various options proposed to deal with it. Then write an essay proposing what you consider the most viable solution to the problem.

Imagine

Choose a profession that interests you and has also been around for a while (law, banking, law enforcement, engineering, government, etc.). Imagine that you are a member of one of these professions and have just come back to Chicago in 1860 after being away for ten years. Describe this new, drier, cleaner world.

1 What do you remember most about the city before the raising of the buildings?   **2** How did this previous condition make it difficult for your particular line of work?   **3** What is the biggest, most obvious change you have noticed upon your return?   **4** What else do you notice?   **5** What happened right away when you went back to work?   **6** What new projects are you now able to take on?   **7** How is your life outside of work affected?   **8** What challenges persist?   **9** How has your business grown?   **10** What other changes are still needed that would be an advantage for you?

Write a letter to your Aunt Nelly back in Boston. Tell her all about your new life in Chicago.

FEBRUARY 1862
CONFEDERATE POWS FILL CAMP DOUGLAS

Five prisoners of war in Confederate uniforms at Camp Douglas Prison. Liljenquist Family Collection of Civil War Photographs (Library of Congress). Available from loc.gov/pictures/item/2012646159, accessed August 20, 2013.

Background

Chicago may have been far from Civil War battlefields, but it was still very much part of the war, supplying food and materials to the troops. Chicago factories made trains that moved the troops. Tens of thousands of Chicagoans fought for the North, and more than 4,000 gave their lives.

Chicago also was the home of Camp Douglas, a prison camp for captured Confederate soldiers. Camp Douglas often housed more than 10,000 prisoners of war at a time, and the conditions were horrific. In the three years that it served as a prison, 4,457 Southerners died, mostly as a result of the wretched sanitary conditions.

Check out the display devoted to the Civil War at the *Chicago: Crossroads of America* exhibit at the Chicago History Museum.

Search online at the Encyclopedia of Chicago on the Chicago History Museum's website to discover more photos, articles, and facts about Camp Douglas and Chicago's role in the Civil War.

Now write a concise summary of the history of Camp Douglas.

Remember

From what you have learned in school, what you have read, and what you have picked up in movies and on TV, what images do the words below produce? Write your reactions to the following:

1 Prisons.   2 Civil War prisons.   3 POWs.   4 Young Confederate soldiers.   5 Confederate officers.   6 Families of Confederate prisoners.   7 Prison food.   8 Prison beds.   9 Guards.   10 Prison gangs.

Combine these images into a description of what you think a Civil War prison camp might have been like.

Go Online

Go to **chicago.writethroughamerica.com/douglas** to access useful links and student writing samples for the Discover and Decide prompts.

Discover

A Shortly after the end of the Civil War, the Chicago chapter of the Fenian Brotherhood, a secret paramilitary organization devoted to overthrowing British rule in Ireland, raised $10,000 and contributed a number of volunteers to participate in an outlandish plan. On June 1, 1866, Irish American veterans of both the Union and Confederate armies launched a short-lived, ill-fated invasion of Canada. Write a report on this little known incident in Chicago history.

B Although no major Civil War battles were fought in Illinois, thousands of Civil War veterans are buried in Chicago cemeteries. Take your camera, tour these sites, and share the details of your trip with your class.

C As a small group project, write a series of monologues or free verse poems based on letters written by the 10 characters listed below in the Imagine section. Then present the collection as a Reader's Theater event.

D Although excavation of the Camp Douglas site is still in the beginning stages, much is being done to bring the Camp Douglas story to the public eye. Students at the Illinois Institute of Technology are creating *Virtual Camp Douglas,* a three-dimensional map of 1864 Camp Douglas that will be superimposed on Google Earth.

Contact the Camp Douglas Restoration Project and conduct an online or phone interview to learn more about the status of the restoration project, and/or arrange to have a member of the foundation come to speak to your class.

Decide

A In the aftermath of the Civil War, an investigation into conditions in Southern POW camps led to the execution of Captain Henry Wirz, the commandant of Andersonville Prison in Georgia. Many historians, however, consider Wirz to have been unjustly convicted and argue that conditions in Northern camps were just as bad, if not worse, than those in Andersonville. Research conditions in Andersonville and Camp Douglas, and write an essay either exonerating Wirz or condemning the commandant of Camp Douglas, Colonel Joseph H. Tucker.

B After the closing of Camp Douglas in 1866, the bodies of 4,000 Confederate prisoners who died there were disinterred and buried in a mass grave at Oak Woods Cemetery in the Hyde Park neighborhood. Today Confederate Mound, along with a monument flanked by four cannons, is designated as a U.S. National Cemetery. Some Chicago aldermen, however, resisted designating the monument as an official city landmark because they felt it honored the Confederacy, a government that advocated black slavery. Research the subject and write an editorial presenting your own opinion on the matter. Strengthen the impact of your essay by incorporating quotes from your peers and teachers.

Imagine

Look at this list of people who could have been at Camp Douglas:

1 Jimmy, a bitterly homesick youth from a desperately poor family.
2 Roger, a proud Confederate officer.   3 Clyde, an exteme racist.
4 Alvin, a potential deserter.   5 Murray, a plantation owner's nephew.
6 Philip, the father of 10.   7 Owen, a medical school student.
8 Michael, a recent emigrant from Ireland.   9 Sidney, a coward.
10 Sebastian, an artist.

Pick one of the people listed above, and in that person's voice write a letter to a close friend or loved one. Describe prison life as you imagine it might be for that person; include the feelings and dreams that person might experience.

MAY 3, 1865
LINCOLN'S FUNERAL TRAIN STOPS IN CHICAGO

"Arch at Twelfth Street, Chicago, President Abraham Lincoln's Hearse and Young Ladies." Photograph by Samuel Montague Fassett (1865, Library of Congress). Available from loc.gov/pictures/item/20086802541, accessed August 20, 2013.

Background

Of the 11 funerals for Abraham Lincoln, Chicago's was perhaps the most impressive. This amazing man, the president who saved the Union, had a special relationship with the city: he practiced law here, campaigned for political office here, and received the nomination for the presidency here. After arriving on a train, his casket was carried to City Hall by a hearse pulled by six black horses. The procession passed under a massive arch erected for the occasion. The huge crowd, many sitting in trees, included 10,000 school children. At City Hall thousands viewed the president in his casket. The next evening, 3,000 torches illuminated the procession back to the train.

Check out displays devoted to Abraham Lincoln at the *Chicago: Crossroads of America* exhibit at the Chicago History Museum.

Search online at the Encyclopedia of Chicago on the Chicago History Museum's website to discover more about Lincoln's Chicago connections.

Now write a concise summary of what you have learned about the journey of Lincoln's funeral train from Washington, D.C., to Springfield, Illinois.

Remember

Recall a meaningful ceremony that you attended. This could have been a funeral, a wedding, a graduation, a surprise party, an award ceremony, or some other event that just worked out as planned.

1 What was the ceremony?   2 Who planned it?   3 Who attended?
4 Why were you there?   5 How did it begin?   6 How did it unfold?
7 How did it conclude?   8 What did you do afterward?   9 What were some typical positive reactions to the ceremony?   10 What images from the ceremony can you still picture?

Describe this ceremony in 150 words or less.

Go Online

Go to chicago.writethroughamerica.com/lincoln to access useful links and student writing samples for the Discover and Decide prompts.

Discover

A Although Lincoln was born in Kentucky and lived for 13 years in Indiana, Illinois proudly bills itself as the "Land of Lincoln." Create a timeline that highlights the key events of Lincoln's years in Illinois.

B Written to commemorate the one-year anniversary of Lincoln's assassination, Walt Whitman's poem "When Lilacs Last in the Dooryard Bloom'd" is a moving tribute to the fallen president. As a small group project, recite Whitman's poem to your class. Try experimenting with solo, dual, and choral voices in your recitation.

C The motion picture *Lincoln* (2012 PG 13) chronicles the last few months of the president's life, ending with his assassination at Ford's Theatre on April 14, 1865. Choosing either a flashback from Lincoln's earlier years in Illinois or the funeral ceremony in Chicago, write an additional scene for the film.

D Visit the Abraham Lincoln Presidential Library and Museum in Springfield, Illinois, and write an article about your experience. Submit the article to your school paper or local newspaper, or post it as a blog on the museum's website.

Decide

A Actor Daniel Day-Lewis's portrayal of Lincoln in 2012 is not the only film treatment of the life of our 16th president. After viewing *Lincoln* (2012 PG 13), watch either *Young Mr. Lincoln* (1939) or *Abe Lincoln in Illinois* (1940). Write an essay comparing and contrasting the strengths of *Lincoln* and one of the other two films.

B Abraham Lincoln's wife, Mary Todd Lincoln, has often been portrayed as more of a hindrance than a help to her husband during his years in office. Learn more about the life of this controversial figure, and write an essay arguing whether or not her unflattering reputation is justified.

Imagine

The day before the funeral, people from all over the city and region decided to attend. Many traveled a distance to Chicago. Others came from close by. This was something that they could not miss. Pretend that you are one of the people planning to attend the Lincoln Chicago funeral. Here are a few possibilities. You are a...

1 Mother who has lost a son in the war.   2 Disabled Union veteran.
3 Highly decorated officer.   4 13-year-old orphan who has lived in the streets most of her life.   5 Free black who lived in Chicago prior to the Civil War.   6 Former slave.   7 Widow whose relatives live in the South.   8 Wealthy banker.   9 Newly arrived emigrant from Germany.   10 Poet.

Write a short explanation of why you are going to be in the crowd. Why does the occasion matter so much to you? Use what you know already about Lincoln, along with credible invented details to make your story come alive.

OCTOBER 8, 1871
FIRE RAGES THROUGH CHICAGO!

Ruins in Chicago, after the great fire of October 1871. Stereograph Cards Collection (Library of Congress). Available from loc.gov/pictures/items/2004682764, accessed August 20, 2013.

Background

On October 8, 1871, a fire started on the Near West Side of the city. Because of the drought conditions, strong winds, and an undermanned fire department, the fire spread rapidly. It raged for 36 hours. Rain finally controlled the fire, but at least 300 people had perished. Three and one-half square miles of downtown Chicago were consumed. In all, 18,000 structures were destroyed. One-third of the population lost their homes.

It was rumored that the fire began in the barn of Mrs. Catherine O'Leary when her cow kicked over a kerosene lamp. But this has never been proved. Other theories have been proposed, but they too have not been verified.

While the cause of the fire remains in question, the response is not. Chicago, with the help of worldwide donations, rebuilt itself remarkably quickly, proving again the energy of its people.

Check out the display devoted to the Great Chicago Fire at the *Chicago: Crossroads of America* exhibit at the Chicago History Museum.

Search online at the Encyclopedia of Chicago on the Chicago History Museum's website to discover more photos, articles, and facts about the event.

Now write a concise summary of the events of the Great Chicago Fire.

Remember

Some events from our past are certain. We know how they started and why and to what effect. Others, like the Chicago Fire, are not so definite. Did the cow do it or not? Recall such an uncertain incident from your life. It happened, but you're not sure why. You might have been in the middle of it or off to the side. But you were there.

1 How old were you? What mattered in your life? 2 Where did this incident take place? 3 How did the incident begin? 4 How did it develop? 5 How did it conclude? 6 What were you doing during all of this? 7 At the time, what seemed to be the cause? 8 As time went by, how did different theories emerge? 9 What explanation was finally accepted? 10 When you look back now, what do you think was the real story?

Write three different versions of this event, each with a different cause and perhaps a different result.

Go Online

Go to **chicago.writethroughamerica.com/chicagofire** to access useful links and student writing samples for the Discover and Decide prompts.

Discover

A Although the most devastating forest fire in recorded North American history, the Great Peshtigo Fire, claimed between 1,200 and 2,400 victims and destroyed millions of dollars worth of property, it received relatively little media attention at the time because Chicago went up in flames on the same night. Learn more about the Great Peshtigo Fire; then write a retrospective article on this "other" fire that occurred on October 8, 1871.

B Although probably not appreciated by the survivors of the fire at the time, the Great Chicago Fire proved to be a catalyst for change in the city of Chicago. Create a poster or PowerPoint presentation displaying the positive impacts the fire had on the development of Chicago.

C Imagine you have been commissioned to write a play about the Great Chicago Fire. First read a review of Lookingglass Theatre's unique dramatic interpretation of the event, *The Great Fire* (2011). Now write a scene for your own play.

D Although the 1937 film treatment of the Great Chicago Fire, *In Old Chicago,* won two Academy Awards and was nominated for four others, it takes considerable liberties with the historical facts of the conflagration. Watch the film and write a review that addresses the strengths and weaknesses of the film's approach.

Decide

A In 1999, The John Marshall Law School staged a mock trial of "Peg Leg" Sullivan, a man considered by some historians to have been the person responsible for starting the Great Chicago Fire. Go online to research this and other theories on the cause of the Great Chicago Fire. Then write an essay using this thesis starter to focus your argument: "The most likely cause of the Great Chicago Fire was ——— because ———."

B The practice of unjustly singling out and blaming an individual or group for negative treatment dates back to the earliest days of recorded time. For years Mrs. Catherine O'Leary and her cow served as perhaps the most famous scapegoats in Chicago history. Investigate some other historical scapegoats; then write an essay determining what these victims had in common.

Imagine

It's easy to imagine how the fire devastated large institutions and important individuals, but it must have had just as big an impact on people who would not be considered newsworthy. Imagine 10 people who did not suffer any personal losses but whose lives were affected dramatically by the fire.

1 Civil War veteran. **2** Skilled laborer. **3** Recently arrived immigrant. **4** Farmer. **5** Teacher. **6** Student. **7** Architect. **8** Police officer. **9** Artist. **10** Spy.

Choose three of these people, and write one diary entry for each of them, describing what he or she experienced in the city during the fire.

MAY 4, 1886
HAYMARKET SQUARE EXPLODES!

The Haymarket Riot. Harper's Weekly (May 15, 1886). Available from chicagohs.org/hadc/visuals/59V0460v.jpg, accessed August 20, 2013.

Background

On May 4, 1886, more than 1,500 people crowded into Haymarket Square. Many were labor activists there to demonstrate against the lockout at McCormick Reaper Works, a manufacturer of heavy farm equipment, and to show their support for universal labor causes such as the eight-hour workday. Also in the crowd were people who were merely curious. Police moved in to break up what had been a peaceful rally. Someone threw a bomb. Seven officers were killed. Shooting followed, and four civilians died.

Check out the display devoted to the Haymarket Riot at the *Chicago: Crossroads of America* exhibit at the Chicago History Museum.

Search online at the Encyclopedia of Chicago at the Chicago History Museum's website to discover more photos, articles, and facts about the Haymarket Riot and subsequent trial.

Now that you have familiarized yourself with the event, write a concise summary of the events of the Haymarket Riot.

Remember

Recall a time when you were part of a large crowd. Try to visualize the event as if it were happening right now.

1 What is your initial reaction to the size of the crowd? Maybe you have several reactions, perhaps even contradictory feelings.   2 Who is at this event?   3 Why are you there?   4 From where you are standing, what can you see? What is out of sight for you?   5 What can you hear? What is out of earshot for you?   6 Is the crowd changing at all? Getting larger? More impatient? Getting smaller?   7 Do you want to leave? If so, why?   8 How concerned are you for your safety? Why? 9 What image of this crowd will stay with you?   10 Do you think that attending this event will change your life? In what way?

Write this as a first-person, present-tense, stream-of-consciousness account.

Go Online

Go to **chicago.writethroughamerica.com/haymarket** to access useful links and student writing samples for the Discover and Decide prompts.

Discover

A Write a three-page report on the Haymarket Riot. Devote one page to the historical context of the riot, one page to the riot itself, and one page to the aftermath and consequences of the riot. Label the sections *Before, During,* and *After.*

B The term "anarchist" conjured strong feelings in 19th century America. Learn more about the role anarchists played in history. Then present a five-minute informative speech or video on the subject.

C Editorial cartoonists argued positions on both sides of the Haymarket Riot controversy. Pick a social or political issue that is relevant today, and design two cartoons—one pro and one con.

D As a small group project, write a series of monologues or free-verse poems using the voices of people connected to the Haymarket Riot. Then present the collection as a Reader's Theater event.

Decide

A In a time when photography was still in its infancy, Americans received their visual impressions of the Haymarket Riot and the subsequent trial from such periodicals as *Frank Leslie's Illustrated News* (see illustration above). Examine Leslie's depictions of the Haymarket Riot. Consider using this thesis starter as a focus for an essay on the objectivity of the media's coverage: "Frank Leslie presented a biased/an unbiased perspective on the Haymarket Riot by…"

B Americans still find occasions to take to the streets to demonstrate against what they perceive as injustice. Consider subjects about which people today get excited, especially those related to youth: What should be taught in school? How should teachers be judged? What are a student's rights? Use this thesis starter to help you write an essay on your own beliefs: "I would be willing to demonstrate over the issue of ——— because…"

Imagine

You are a young reporter gathering quotes for a newspaper article about the Haymarket Demonstration. Although you managed to interview people, you left before the violence erupted. You met a/an...

1 Advocate of the eight-hour workday.   2 Critic of the strikebreakers.
3 Pacifist.   4 Skilled laborer recently arrived from Scotland.
5 Artist.   6 Aide to the mayor.   7 Policeman.   8 Clergyman.
9 Factory owner.   10 Private detective.

Write an article capturing the mood of the crowd before the violence began. Start with a lead paragraph. Use all of your quotes from the people you interviewed. You know what happened later; this is to capture the mood before the bombing and gunfire.

1889
JANE ADDAMS ESTABLISHES HULL HOUSE

Jane Adams, *c.* 1914. (Library of Congress). Available from loc.gov/pictures/item/2004671949, accessed August 20, 2013.

Background

In 1889 Jane Addams, a wealthy, 29-year-old woman from Rockford, Illinois, established Hull House in the slums of Chicago. Its purpose was to help the people from that neighborhood—mostly recent immigrants—cope with life and create better futures for themselves. Hull House offered day care; kindergarten classes; instruction in cooking, sewing, and citizenship; a lending library; and other cultural experiences. Jane Addams and most of her staff lived at Hull House.

Check out the display devoted to Jane Addams at the *Chicago: Crossroads of America* exhibit at the Chicago History Museum.

Search online at the Encyclopedia of Chicago on the Chicago History Museum's website to discover more photos, articles, and facts about Jane Addams and Hull House.

Now write a concise summary of the history of Hull House.

Remember

Recall a time when you had a problem that you solved with the generous help of someone else. This may not have been a problem on the scale of those faced by the people living near Hull House, but it did concern you, and you were grateful when this problem was no longer in your life.

1 How old were you at the time? What was going on in your life?
2 What was the problem you faced?   3 Why did it happen when it did?   4 What would have happened if you had not solved the problem?   5 Who came to your aid?   6 Why did this person decide to assist you?   7 What in particular did this person do for you?   8 What was the immediate result of these efforts?   9 How was the problem finally solved?   10 How important was this event in your life?

Shape your answers into a personal narrative. Address it to people who regard accepting help as a sign of weakness. Using your story as an example, try to convince these people that total independence is neither possible nor desirable.

Go Online

Go to **chicago.writethroughamerica.com/jaddams** to access useful links and student writing samples for the Discover and Decide prompts.

Discover

A Visit the Chicago History Museum and study the Jane Addams display in the *Chicago: Crossroads of America* exhibit. Write down what you find interesting, surprising, and obvious. What further questions does this information raise?

B Create a PowerPoint presentation on how other reformers, such as Ellen Gates Starr, helped Jane Addams and how people like Julia Lathrop continued what Jane Addams began.

C Learn more about the extensive opportunities that Hull House offered the community in the areas of theater and athletics. Create a series of posters celebrating the rich past of Hull House:

D Visit the Jane Addams Hull-House Museum on 800 South Halsted Street. Bring a video camera and create a one-minute commercial to attract visitors to the museum.

Decide

A Would you have been a good candidate for living and working at Hull House? In your answer explain your strengths and your interests. A visit to the Hull-House Museum will lend perspective.

B Write a review of Lucy Knight's biography of Jane Addams. What does this add to your knowledge of the person and the period? What questions does it answer? What questions remain?

Imagine

Pretend you are one of the young people who moved to Hull House to help Jane Addams. You are capable, motivated, and serious, but this is still a new and challenging experience for you.

1 Who are you? How did you hear about Hull House? Why did you decide to become involved?   2 Explain why you recommend a sewing class for the first person you meet.   3 The second person, an older Italian lady, is quite angry. Explain the cause of her anger and your solution.   4 You take a break to visit the pottery class. What is that like? 5 Right before lunch a mother and two children appear. What does the mother say she wants? What do you suggest instead?   6 At lunch, you talk to another young person working at Hull House. He has decided to leave. What are his reasons?   7 In the afternoon, you fail to help someone, and she stalks out. What happens next?   8 In the late afternoon Jane Addams meets with the staff. What does she discuss?   9 You stay after the meeting and ask her some questions. What do you ask? What are her responses?   10 After dinner, you take a walk in an area you have never visited. It is even more desperate than what you have seen before. What is it like?

Use your answers to these questions as the basis for a day-in-the-life account of your early days working for Jane Addams. Write this as a letter to a friend, someone who will enjoy hearing about your new life. Describe places and people whenever possible.

1893
BLACK SURGEON PIONEERS TECHNIQUE

Daniel Hale Williams, c. 1900. Available from Wikimedia Commons file: Daniel_Hale_Williams.jpg, accessed August 20, 2013.

Background

Daniel Hale Williams was a remarkable man. He was one of the very first physicians to perform open-heart pericardial surgery, and he did it in 1893 without the benefit of penicillin or blood transfusions. His patient, James Cornish, who suffered from a knife wound, recovered completely and went on to live a normal life.

Dr. Williams performed the surgery at Provident Hospital, which he had founded because white hospitals offered limited opportunites to African American doctors. Later, he moved to Washington, D.C., to continue his distinguished medical career. Dr. Williams's medical and administrative skills were extraordinary, and his tireless efforts made it possible for African Americans to enjoy better health care than they ever had experienced before.

Check out the display devoted to Dr. Daniel Hale Williams at the DuSable Museum of African American History.

Visit the International Museum of Surgical Science at 1524 North Lake Shore Drive to discover more about Chicago's early medical history.

Now that you have familiarized yourself with the facts about Dr. Daniel Hale Williams, write a concise summary of his accomplishments.

Remember

When the time came, Daniel Hale Williams performed admirably in difficult conditions. Recall a time that you succeeded against harsh odds. This was a proud moment for you.

1 How old were you at the time?   2 What was the challenge?
3 Why was it so difficult?   4 What would have happened if you had chosen not to meet the challenge?   5 What was your plan for success?
6 How did you begin?   7 What was the most difficult step as you tried to complete the task?   8 How did you finally do it?   9 How did you feel immediately afterward?   10 When you look back, how do you view this accomplishment?

Write this as a personal narrative, but start near the middle—at the critical moment. Use a flashback to fill in the essential details.

Go Online

Go to **chicago.writethroughamerica.com/dhwilliams** to access useful links and student writing samples for the Discover and Decide prompts.

Discover

A Create a timeline or PowerPoint presentation of the evolution of heart surgery from the days of Dr. Daniel Hale Williams to the present.

B Using plenty of dialogue interspersed with narration, write the script to a one-act play or Reader's Theater performance based upon Dr. Williams's historic operation, and present it to your class.

C Using the first-person voice of Dr. Daniel Hale Williams, write a free-verse poem, rap, or monologue about Williams's fateful decision to perform open-heart surgery. Try experimenting with an unfamiliar format.

D The DuSable Museum of African American History brings history to life. Visit the museum to learn more about other notable African Americans who were pioneers in their fields. Write an article about your visit and submit it to your school's newspaper.

Decide

A Rather than looking to successful professionals such as Daniel Hale Williams, young people instead often idolize celebrities and sports figures. Can this be harmful? Investigate the issue, and write an essay outlining the dangers of using celebrity figures as role models.

B Although non-whites account for more than 25 percent of the population, only 6 percent of practicing physicians in the United States are people of color. Investigate the situation and write an editorial about what can be done to increase the number of minority students in medical school.

Imagine

Williams's story illustrates that even though the Civil War had ended and even though Chicago was in the North, African Americans were not given equal treatment. Imagine that you are a young and talented member of a minority group, and you decide to move to a place with opportunities—but a place where many do not treat you equally. You will succeed in this challenging environment, but it will not be easy.

1 What is your special skill? How did you acquire it?   2 Where do you plan to move?   3 Why will this place give you so many opportunities?   4 Of what minority group are you a member?   5 How are you treated badly in your first encounters in this new place?   6 How do you react to this first rejection?   7 How do you react when you continue to experience rejection?   8 How do you finally start to make a breakthrough?   9 How do you continue to have more success?
10 How does this impact your later career?

Shape these responses into an inspirational speech you will deliver to a local high school. The title of the speech is "Don't Quit!"

OCTOBER 9, 1893
WORLD'S FAIR DRAWS RECORD CROWD

Four boys posed at World's Columbian Exposition, Chicago. Photograph by Frances Benjamin Johnston. Johnston Collection (Library of Congress). Available from loc.gov/pictures/item/92501023, accessed August 20, 2013.

Background

On October 9, 1893, 716,881 people traveled to Chicago's South Side to visit the Columbian Exposition for "Chicago Day." This was the biggest single-event crowd ever. The fair covered 600 acres. It had 200 buildings, some featuring different countries and states and others displaying the most recent advances in science. There was a Ferris wheel with 36 cars, each able to carry 60 people. There were canals and a train and musical shows and lots of food. When the fair closed six months after it opened, twenty million people had visited.

The planning and work that went into building this fair, which honored the 400th birthday of Christopher Columbus's landing, was extensive. The work was made harder by the fact that the architects, artists, and financial supporters did not always agree with one another. But somehow they found a way to get the job done.

Check out the display devoted to the World's Columbian Exposition at the *Chicago: Crossroads of America* exhibit at the Chicago History Museum.

Search online at the Encyclopedia of Chicago on the Chicago History Museum's website to discover more photos, articles, and facts about the fair.

Now write a concise summary of the main events of the World's Columbian Exposition.

Remember

Recall a time when you were so excited about attending an event that nothing else mattered to you as you counted down the days for the event to arrive.

1 How old were you?   2 What was the event? A circus? Fair? Baseball game? Play?   3 How did you first hear about the event?   4 How was the event promoted? Posters? TV ads?   5 As the event got closer, how did you get ready? What did others think of your excitement? 6 What did you do the day before the event? Were you able to sleep? 7 When you finally got to go, what did you find to be the most predictable aspect of the event?   8 What was the most surprising aspect of the event?   9 Overall, were you disappointed or pleased?   10 As you recall the event now, what details stand out the most?

Write a short piece explaining what a big day this was for you. Address this to someone who does not understand its importance.

Go Online

Go to **chicago.writethroughamerica.com/worldsfair** to access useful links and student writing samples for the Discover and Decide prompts.

Discover

A When George Ferris built the first "Ferris Wheel," Chicago considered itself to have an architectural wonder on a par with the Eiffel Tower in Paris. A mere 13 years later, however, the wheel's owners spent considerable time and effort destroying it with dynamite. Research the history of this innovative contraption and write a report on its brief, yet colorful, life span.

B The World's Columbian Exposition served as a showcase for a number of new products, including "Candied Popcorn and Peanuts"—America's favorite caramel corn treat now known as Cracker Jack®. Investigate what other products debuted at the exposition; then create a PowerPoint presentation about them and present it to your class.

C Design a poster advertising the World's Columbian Exposition. Decide whether you wish to focus on one particular exhibit or to present a spectrum of "wonders."

D Erik Larson's *The Devil in the White City* is a nonfiction account of the World's Columbian Exposition. Written in a novelistic style, the book merges the stories of both Daniel Burnham, the chief architect of the fair, and Dr. Henry Howard Holmes, a serial killer who murdered several visitors to the fair. Watch the award-winning documentary *H.H. Holmes: America's First Serial Killer*. A film version of Larson's book is in the works, with Leonardo DiCaprio playing the role of Dr. Holmes. Based on what you have learned from the documentary and what you know of DiCaprio's roles, write a one-paragraph essay supporting your own choice for casting Holmes's role.

Decide

A Many African Americans believed that they were poorly represented at the World's Columbian Exposition. Prominent activist Frederick Douglass stated that the model African villages were designed "to exhibit the Negro as a repulsive savage," and anti-lynching activist Ida B. Wells wrote a treatise on the subject. Investigate the role of African Americans in the Exposition and argue either for or against these two activists' positions.

B Although the number of African American characters on television programs has increased significantly since the early days of television, some people argue that the media depiction of African Americans presents a stereotypical picture of black men and women. Read some articles on the subject and watch some television programs that depict African Americans. Then write a position paper either attacking or defending television's role in race relations.

Imagine

You are the principal of a troubled school in a struggling neighborhood, but you have an idea for making things better: a mini world's fair with 20 exhibits celebrating the talents and interests of students and members of the community. The fair is a success, largely because of you.

1 How did you convince the school board that their doubts about the project were unfounded?   **2** How did you decide to raise money?
3 Two people who offered to be your assistant liked the idea but hated each other. Why? How did you resolve that problem?   **4** You planned to hold the event in the gym, but Coach Roberts would not permit all of those people on his new gym floor. What did you do?   **5** Various social and ethnic groups submitted plans for exhibits celebrating their cultures, but you needed to simplify them. How did you succeed?
6 How did you get reluctant people from the community to participate?   **7** The local paper was going to cover the event, but the reporter was to be Jake Plutarch, a young man you expelled 14 years ago. Was this a problem?   **8** Your son called from London. He needed to see you right away. How did this affect your plans?   **9** Madame Foch, the head of the language department, felt slighted at not having been consulted. What did you say to her?   **10** The poster announcing the event had a typo. What did you do?

Years later, your grandson asks, "How did you do it, Gramps?" Write down what you told him. Try to capture your feelings as well as your decisions.

MAY 11, 1894
PULLMAN WORKERS STRIKE!

Pullman strikers outside Arcade Building in Pullman, Chicago, 1894. Abraham Lincoln Historical Digitization Project (Chicago Historical Society). Available from Wikimedia Commons file: Pullman-strike.djvu, accessed August 20, 2013.

Background

Chicago, like most big cities, has had its share of labor–management confrontations. Perhaps the most infamous and most costly was the strike at the Pullman Palace Car Company, a large company that manufactured railroad cars. On May 11, 1894, about 4,000 workers walked off the job protesting recently lowered wages. Even though the workers lived in housing provided by the company, there was no corresponding reduction in rent. This walkout led to the involvement of a national union, a national boycott of all trains that carried Pullman cars, the dispatch of federal troops to town, and, then, the jailing of the union leader. When the strike was finally settled, the union had lost most of its demands but had gained support from the American public and government.

Check out the display devoted to the Pullman Strike at the Historic Pullman State Historic Site at 11111 South Forrestville Avenue.

Search online at the Encyclopedia of Chicago at the Chicago History Museum's website to discover more about this acrimonious conflict.

Now write a concise summary of the events and aftermath of the 1894 Pullman Strike.

Remember

Labor disputes like the Pullman Strike involve people who are strong-minded, principled, and stubborn. They put what they believe into action. They take risks. Who is a person you have met or you have heard of that fits this description? Think of…

1 Relatives.   2 Friends.   3 Teachers.   4 Adults in your community.
5 An ancestor.   6 Religious figures.   7 Political figures.   8 Athletes.
9 Characters in books.   10 Characters in movies.

Write a short profile of this individual. How does this person demonstrate his or her strong convictions?

Go Online

Go to **chicago.writethroughamerica.com/pullman** to access useful links and student writing samples for the Discover and Decide prompts.

Discover

A *And the sons of Pullman porters and the sons of engineers*
They ride their fathers' magic carpet made of steam.
Mothers with their babes asleep are rockin' to the gentle beat;
The rhythm of the rails is all they dream.
(Steve Goodman, "City of New Orleans")

Folksinger Steve Goodman wrote "City of New Orleans" on a notepad while on board one of the train's trips. The song went on to become one of the most popular train songs ever written. Learn more about the "City of New Orleans." Then write a tribute article about the train, the song, and this native Chicagoan who won a posthumous Grammy Award for it.

B The 1894 Pullman Strike that started with 4,000 men in the Pullman neighborhood spread to include more than 100,000 workers in 27 states. Eugene Debs, the president of the American Railway Union (ARU), was eventually jailed for six months for his role in the strike. Assuming the persona of Debs, write and deliver a two-minute speech urging railroad workers to join their brothers in Pullman in the strike. Use both emotion *(pathos)* and reasoning *(logos)* in your appeal.

C Although the strike of 1894 tarnished his reputation, George Pullman had envisioned the creation of a town for his workers that was both socially progressive and profitable. Create a blueprint of a model town of your own, and write a one-page synopsis of your vision.

D The Historic Pullman Foundation offers tours of the Pullman neighborhood. Take your camera and check out the Visitor Center, or take a tour of the Pullman neighborhood. Make a video or PowerPoint presentation of the experience and share it with others.

Decide

A In the fall of 2012 the Chicago Teachers Union went on strike for nine days. One of the points of contention between the union and the school board was the criteria used in teacher evaluations. Research the issue of teacher evaluation and write an essay in which you set forth a proposal for an appropriate method to evaluate teachers. Consider using quotes from teachers, administrators, students, and parents to substantiate your argument.

B Although countries in Europe and Asia have been using high-speed commuter trains for years, progress on the United States' plan to follow suit has been slow to develop. Research President Obama's plan to develop a high-speed rail system and write an essay arguing either for against his plan to spend $53 billion on the project.

Imagine

Consider this plot summary of an event: "Workers and management at Acme, Inc., make concessions, and the strike is finally over."

Expand this into a news story, but first add more details:

1 What does Acme do? Why is the company important? **2** Why do the Acme workers go on strike? **3** What early offer by management do the workers reject? **4** What happens when management brings in strikebreakers? **5** What offer by the workers does management reject? **6** How is the city affected by the strike? **7** How are the families of the workers affected? **8** How is the strike finally brought to an end? **9** What are some of the immediate consequences of the strike? **10** What are some of the long-term consequences?

Remember that the lead paragraph should answer the questions: who, what, when, where, why, and how.

1896
DEWEY OPENS EXPERIMENTAL SCHOOL

John Dewey, 1902. Original photograph from the John Dewey Photograph Collection, Morris Library, Southern Illinois University at Carbondale. Available from Wikimedia Commons file: John_Dewey_in_1902.jpg, accessed August 20, 2013.

Background

John Dewey was the leader of a movement whose members believed that schools should be active places where students learn by doing and as a result become more active citizens.

In 1896, Dewey started the University of Chicago Laboratory Schools. Its purpose was to carry out his ideas of active learning. This was one of the first schools in the country to be based entirely on this progressive philosophy.

Check out the display devoted to progressive education at the Winnetka Public Library.

Search online at the Encyclopedia of Chicago on the Chicago History Museum's website to discover more photos, articles, and facts about progressive education and John Dewey.

Now write a concise summary of the accomplishments of John Dewey.

Remember

When did you learn something in school by discovering it yourself? Describe the whole experience:

1 How old were you at the time? 2 Who was the teacher? Did this teacher encourage discovery learning? 3 What was going on the day you made the discovery? 4 What were you supposed to learn that day? 5 Why was this supposed to be important? 6 Did you consider it important or not? 7 How did the learning start? 8 How was the lesson completed? 9 What was your immediate reaction to all of this? 10 When did you first realize that something quite important had happened?

Recapture this past event by writing about it in the present tense, perhaps in a diary or letter form.

Go Online

Go to **chicago.writethroughamerica.com/jdewey** to access useful links and student writing samples for the Discover and Decide prompts.

Discover

A What was a typical Chicago school like at the time Dewey started his school? Write a day-in-the-life report on Chicago schools at the end of the 19th century.

B Some high schools have switched to a 12-month academic calendar. Investigate this trend in education and present your findings in a speech.

C Write a song or rap dedicated to your favorite teacher and share it with the class—possibly on Teacher Appreciation Day, May 7th.

D Which film best captures the feeling of high school life? *Freedom Writers? Mr. Holland's Opus? Ten Things I Hate About You?* Something else? Compile a list of criteria for an effective school film. Then view two or more films set in high schools, and compare them in terms of your expectations.

Decide

A What qualities does a great teacher possess? Combine online research, interviews with classmates and teachers, and personal experiences into an essay on the subject.

B While some educators and civic leaders view charter schools as the answer to boosting student performance in low-achieving schools, others view charter schools as the undemocratic abandoning of the traditional public-school system. Write an essay taking a stand on this trend in American public education.

Imagine

Imagine that you have been asked to evaluate a 6th-grade class at the University of Chicago Lab Schools. You must determine if the students are learning by discovery and if what they are learning will make them more positive and productive citizens of a democracy. It turns out the class is a terrific example of Dewey's philosophy in action.

What did you like so much about the…

1 Teacher's attitude?   2 The classroom layout?   3 The schedule?
4 The books?   5 The approach to science?   6 The use of the daily
newspaper?   7 Field trips?   8 Guest speakers?   9 Social studies
discussions?   10 Homework?

Write a report to Mr. Dewey telling him why this class proved to be such a good example of progressive education. Add other details to make your case even stronger.

OCTOBER 9, 1906
ALL-CHICAGO WORLD SERIES!

1906 World Series. Boston Public Library: McGreevey Collection. Available from Wikimedia Commons file: Pick-off_attempt_at_ first_1906_World_Series.jpg, accessed August 20, 2013.

Background

On October 9, 1906, for the first time ever the World Series featured two teams from the same city. The powerful Chicago Cubs finished the season with a record-setting 116 wins against 36 losses—20 games ahead of their nearest rival. The Chicago White Sox, known as "The Hitless Wonders," climbed up from sixth place to first place by winning 19 consecutive games. The Cubs were heavily favored to win the World Series, but this was Chicago baseball where anything could happen. The White Sox surprised sports fans by taking the Series, four games to two.

Check out the display devoted to Chicago Baseball at the *Chicago: Crossroads of America* exhibit at the Chicago History Museum.

Search online at the Encyclopedia of Chicago on the Chicago History Museum's website to discover more photos, articles, and facts about the Cubs, the White Sox, and the 1906 matchup.

Now that you have familiarized yourself with the events, write a concise summary of the 1906 World Series.

Remember

What was the most exciting sporting event or competition you have ever witnessed?

1 What was important to you at the time? 2 What was the event? How did it rank with others that you had seen previously? 3 How much waiting was involved before the event took place? 4 Why had you become a fan? Did your family have anything to do with your interest? 5 What did you do the day of the game? How did you prepare? 6 With whom did you sit? 7 What was the atmosphere like before the game? 8 How did the game begin? 9 How did the game develop and end? 10 As you look back, what do you remember the most clearly?

Write this as a letter to a friend who regrets missing the game. Make it as exciting as possible. Recreate what it was like to be a spectator at the event.

Go Online

Go to **chicago.writethroughamerica.com/worldseries** to access useful links and student writing samples for the Discover and Decide prompts.

Discover

A Charles Comiskey, owner of the Chicago White Sox from 1900 to 1931, was so frugal that he held his players responsible for washing their own uniforms. Read more about this man whose teams won five American League championships, and present what you've learned in a one-page character sketch.

B Although the Cubs have been North Siders since their move to Clark and Addison in 1916, the 1906 home of the Chicago Cubs was the West Side Grounds. Create a PowerPoint presentation on the various home parks of the two local ball clubs.

C The poem "Tinkers to Evers to Chance" is considered a classic of its type:
These are the saddest of possible words:
"Tinker to Evers to Chance."
Trio of bear cubs, and fleeter than birds,
Tinker and Evers and Chance.
Ruthlessly pricking our gonfalon bubble,
Making a Giant hit into a double —
Words that are heavy with nothing but trouble:
"Tinker to Evers to Chance."
(Franklin Pierce Adams)
Write an eight-line poem of your own paying tribute to a contemporary hero of yours.

D The second part of Ken Burns's nine-part documentary series *Baseball* includes a segment on the 1906 World Series. Watch the program and write a review.

Decide

A Write a position piece agreeing or disagreeing with cultural historian Jacques Barzun's statement: "Whoever wants to know the heart and mind of America had better learn baseball...." Consider such aspects as rules, fan behavior, pace of the game, and media coverage.

B Many Chicago baseball fans believe that it is impossible to be both a Cubs fan and a White Sox fan, insisting that you can only be one or the other. Interview fans of both teams, and write an essay using the following thesis starter: "It is possible/impossible to be both a Cubs fan and a Sox fan because…"

Imagine

The excitement in Chicago surrounding the 1906 World Series tells us that our current obsession with sports is not unique. It's been around a long time here and elsewhere. It gives plenty for people to talk about and poets to write about, even though it is only a game. Things that ultimately don't matter, matter quite a lot. Understanding fans in 1906 is much like understanding fans today. Life might have been very different in 1906, but people still talked about the Sox and Cubs. Write a roundtable discussion among several people. Some love sports, some find them stupid, and others have no opinion.

Choose four or five panelists from the list or add some others.

1 Yoga instructor   2 Librarian   3 Former All-American linebacker
4 English teacher   5 Neighborhood organizer   6 Coach
7 Police officer   8 Historian   9 Hermit   10 Advertising executive

1906
THE JUNGLE EXPOSES STOCKYARD HORRORS

Scene in the Great Union Stockyards, Chicago *c.* 1900. Stereograph Cards Collection (Library of Congress). Available from loc.gov/pictures/item/20066867971, accessed August 20, 2013.

Background

By the late 1800s, the Union Stock Yards had become one of the giant centers of business activity in Chicago. Miles of railroad tracks converged here. More than 25,000 people, mostly immigrants, worked in the stockyards, slaughtering almost 12 million animals a year.

In the early 1900s, social activist Upton Sinclair decided to write a novel about the stockyards. For research, he went undercover as an employee at a meatpacking company. Working close-up, he found countless vivid examples of a dirty, dangerous, dehumanizing workplace. When his book came out in 1906, it shocked the entire nation and infuriated the owners of the meatpacking companies. But their anger did not stop the passage of new laws that made life better, safer, and cleaner for the workers and assured the consumer of a safer product.

Check out the display devoted to the Chicago stockyards at the *Chicago: Crossroads of America* exhibit at the Chicago History Museum.

Search online at the Encyclopedia of Chicago on the Chicago History Museum's website to discover more photos, articles, and facts about *The Jungle* and the meatpacking industry.

Now write a concise summary of what you have discovered about the Chicago meatpacking industry in the early 1900s.

Remember

Sinclair created a world with an almost overpowering personality—a chaotic, dangerous, exciting, degrading, bloody place. Chances are you have never been in places such as the slaughterhouses Sinclair described, but you have been to places with strong personalities. Recall one of these and describe it. Here are some possible place "personalities":

1 Lonely. 2 Structured. 3 Exciting. 4 Religious. 5 Threatening.
6 Lively. 7 Inspiring. 8 Silly. 9 Tasteful. 10 Futuristic.

Escort your reader through this place, stopping along the way to point out revealing details.

Go Online

Go to **chicago.writethroughamerica.com/jungle** to access useful links and student writing samples for the Discover and Decide prompts.

Discover

A Few books have ever had as immediate an impact as *The Jungle*. Within a year of its publication in 1906, a government investigation had been launched, and the Pure Food and Drug Act and the Meat Inspection Act were enacted. Write a report on the changes in American society prompted by Sinclair's novel.

B Upton Sinclair and his fellow journalists devoted themselves to exposing unsavory business and government practices to the American public. Known as the "muckrakers," their work was instrumental in bringing about much-needed social reform. Read about contemporary investigative journalists, and create a PowerPoint presentation on the muckrakers of today.

C A found poem takes words and phrases from a nonpoetic source and arranges them into an original poem. Using a passage from *The Jungle* for source material, write a found poem that creates a vivid emotional or sensory image.

D Published in the same year as *The Jungle*, Jack London's short story "The Apostate" showed readers a glimpse of the horrors faced by mill workers caught in a hopeless cycle of poverty. Read London's story and write a report on the conditions it exposed to the American public.

Decide

A As opposed to the philosophers in ancient Greece, who attempted to discover the nature of truth, the Sophists were a group of intellectuals who trained themselves to argue either side of a philosophic argument. Take a sophistic approach to the question: "Is it ethically right or wrong to eat meat?" Write a one-page argument in favor of vegetarianism; then write a one-page counterargument against it.

B The neighborhood surrounding the original stockyards is known as the Back of the Yards—the setting for Sinclair's *The Jungle*. The Back of the Yards Neighborhood Council was founded in 1939 to help organize community efforts to deal with social problems and to foster a spirit of solidarity in the community. Visit the Council's office or website and write an article on the work being done today to help the residents of the Back of the Yards.

Imagine

Imagine that you are a worker in a factory that has little concern for its employees. The work is dangerous, dirty, and boring. This is a truly miserable place to work.

1 What is this place? What is manufactured here?   **2** Describe the specific room or area where you work. Why is it so dirty?   **3** Why is it so dangerous?   **4** Why are your particular tasks so boring?   **5** What rules make the place particularly unpleasant?   **6** How is the boss?   **7** How are the people who work with you?   **8** What is unpleasant about lunchtime?   **9** Why don't you quit?   **10** What would happen if you and your fellow workers went on strike?

Write a first-person, present-tense account of one day at this wretched place.

1909
BURNHAM UNVEILS PLAN OF CHICAGO

Plan of Chicago: Civic Center, 1908. Photographic reproduction of original work by Jules Guerin (delineator) and Edward Herbert Bennett and Daniel Hudson Burnham (architects). Available from Wikimedia Commons file: Delineator-_Jules_Guerin:_Architects-_Edward_Herbert_Bennett_and_ Daniel_Hudson_Burnham_-Plan_of_Chicago-_Civic_Center_-_Google_Art_ Project.jpg, accessed August 20, 2013.

Background

Architect Daniel Burnham once said, "Make no little plans," and he meant what he said. He led the group of architects, artists, and engineers who built the Columbian Exposition. In the early 20th century his architectural firm had grown into the largest in the world.

In 1909 he was commissioned to write the *Plan of Chicago* to articulate his vision for the future of the city. What he produced included illustrations; maps; and diagrams of the parks, lakefront, and boulevards. It was widely studied. A simplified version was read by Chicago school children. Not all of his plans were followed, but many were. Historians consider Daniel Burnham to be one of America's first modern city planners.

Check out the display devoted to Daniel Burnham at the *Chicago: Crossroads of America* exhibit at the Chicago History Museum.

Search online at the Encyclopedia of Chicago on the Chicago History Museum's website to discover more photos, articles, and facts about Daniel Burnham and his dream for Chicago.

Now write a concise summary of what you have learned about this architectural visionary.

Remember

It is the task of city planners to decide what must be done now to help the city to continue to grow in the future. Look at these 10 areas that might matter to city planners:

1 Parks   2 Streets and traffic   3 Transportation   4 Libraries
5 Statues and fountains   6 Stadiums   7 Zoos   8 Bike and hiking
trails   9 Museums   10 Security

According to your own experience, which of these is most essential to a city's health? Which is least essential? Explain why you ranked one so high and one so low.

Go Online

Go to **chicago.writethroughamerica.com/burnham** to access useful links and student writing samples for the Discover and Decide prompts.

Discover

A The sketches of artist Jules Guerin helped the public imagine what Daniel Burnham had in mind for Chicago. In addition to his acclaimed renderings of Burnham's *Plan of Chicago,* Guerin was also well respected for his work as an illustrator and muralist. Research the life and work of this artist and write a report on his accomplishments.

B Design a PowerPoint presentation of Daniel Burnham's *Plan of Chicago.* Then use the first-person voice to present the plan to your class as if you yourself were Daniel Burnham.

C Imagine that it is the year 2100. In order to deal with the increasing problem of overpopulation in the city, the Chicago City Planning Commission has decided to expand the city's boundaries by constructing a 10-square-mile underwater neighborhood enclosed under a protective bubble on the floor of Lake Michigan. You and each of your classmates have been offered the opportunity to present your designs in a competition for the first underwater city of the future. Design the layout of the area, and present an argument as to why your firm should win the city contract for the project.

D Take a trip to the Art Institute of Chicago or take a virtual tour on its website to observe the collection of Jules Guerin's watercolor renderings of Daniel Burnham's *Plan of Chicago.* Write a journal entry recounting your reactions to Burnham's visions for the city.

Decide

A Write an essay using this thesis starter: "Chicagoans should be grateful for the vision of Daniel Burnham because…"

B What should Chicago do to ensure that it continues to improve? Make a list of 10 specific priorities that the city needs to accomplish to remain a great city for generations to come. After each point, write a short explanation to justify its importance.

Imagine

Pretend that you are in charge of building a new medium-sized public high school. You have the money and the time and the people to build just what you want.

Draw a map of this perfect school. Make sure you include the...

1 Entrance to the building.   **2** Athletic fields.   **3** Halls.
4 Science labs.   **5** Classrooms.   **6** Study areas.   **7** Media center.
8 Gym.   **9** Cafeteria.   **10** Conference rooms.

Briefly explain what would make each of these fit your plan.

JULY 24, 1915
S.S. EASTLAND CAPSIZES!
844 LOST!

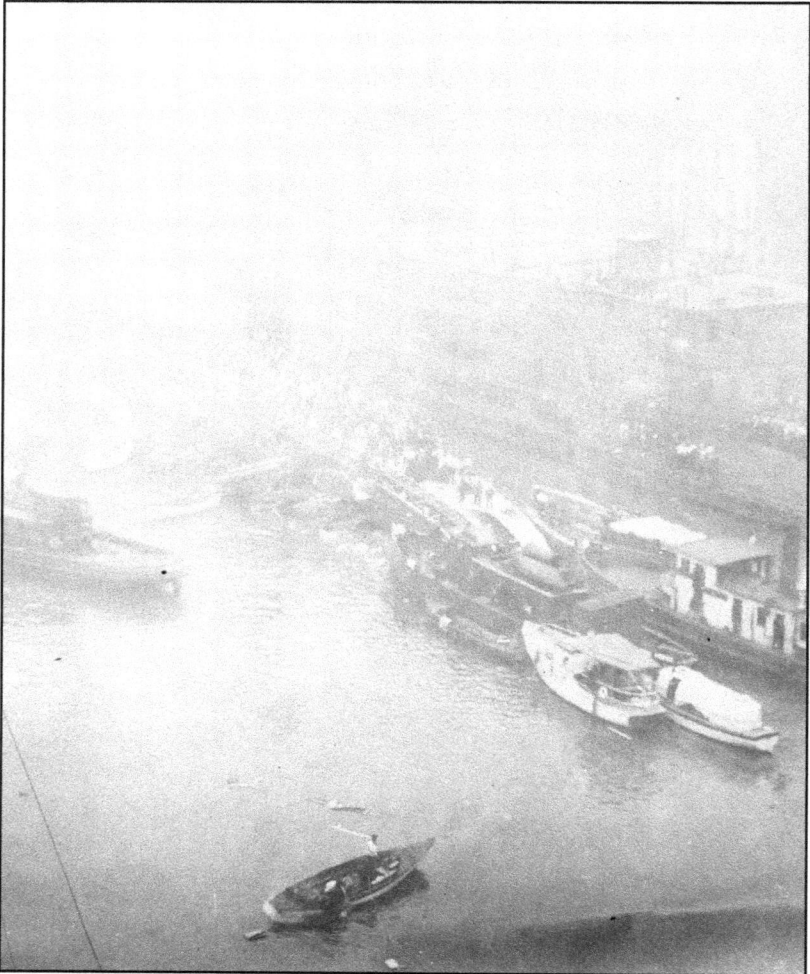

"*Eastland* Overturned in Chicago River, July 24, 1915." George Grantham Bain Collection (Library of Congress). Available from loc.gov/pictures/item/ggb2005019611, accessed August 20, 2013.

Background

On July 24, 1915, The Western Electric Company of Hawthorne Works (now Cicero), Illinois, hired three excursion boats to take company employees and family members for a holiday boat ride and picnic. However, one of the three ships, the S.S. *Eastland,* was both top-heavy and dangerously overloaded. As it cast off, the ship tipped over. Thousands of horrified onlookers watched helplessly as 844 of the 2,500 passengers aboard were drowned within yards of the dock in the greatest loss of life in any disaster in Chicago history.

Check out the display devoted to the *Eastland* disaster at the *Chicago: Crossroads of America* exhibit at the Chicago History Museum.

Browse the *Eastland* Memorial Society's web page.

Now that you have familiarized yourself with the sinking of the S.S. *Eastland,* write a concise summary of the tragedy.

Remember

A few of the *Eastland* passengers chose to act bravely and save the lives of others. Few of us are ever called upon to act with such courage, but we do make choices that carry some risk. Recall a time when you chose to be brave in an adverse situation.

1 How old were you at the time? What was important in your life?
2 What were you expecting to do that particular day?   3 What was the situation? How could this happen?   4 What was your initial reaction to the crisis?   5 What was the easiest choice that you made?
6 What was the more courageous choice?   7 Why was the brave choice so risky? What did you have to lose?   8 How successful were you?   9 How did this action affect your life at that time?   10 When you look back, are you pleased with yourself for having made that choice?

Give this event a title and write a personal narrative. Start in the middle and then use flashbacks to explain why you were in this situation.

Go Online

Go to **chicago.writethroughamerica.com/eastland** to access useful links and student writing samples for the Discover and Decide prompts.

Discover

A Go online to view archive photos of the *Eastland* disaster. Pick five images. For each write a haiku or a caption that captures the mood of the photograph.

B In the summer of 1915, George Halas was a 20-year-old University of Illinois student working at Western Electric and playing sports for the company teams. Although he had bought a ticket for the *Eastland* outing, he arrived too late to be aboard at the time of the tragedy. Learn about Halas's life. Then write a one-page speech and/or PowerPoint presentation detailing the contributions that George Halas made to Chicago.

C One of the true heroes of the *Eastland* disaster was "The Human Frog," Reginald Bowles, who repeatedly dove down and single-handedly recovered the bodies of more than 40 victims. Learn about this 17-year-old's remarkable courage and write a poem, song, or rap in tribute to him.

D How should the victims of the *Eastland* disaster be memorialized? Design your own tribute to the victims of the tragedy. Then write a letter to the mayor of Chicago outlining your proposal and arguing the appropriateness of your concept.

Decide

A Although the sinking of the R.M.S. *Titanic* in 1912 is one of the most infamous disasters in history, the S.S. *Eastland* capsizing just three years later remains relatively unknown. Investigate the two disasters and determine why the first has received so much more attention than the second.

Complete this sentence starter to form your thesis: "The legacy of the R.M.S. *Titanic* sinking has overshadowed the S.S. *Eastland* disaster because…"

B How responsible was Captain Harry Pedersen for the sinking of the S.S. *Eastland?* Research the matter and write an essay arguing either the case for or against Pedersen.

Imagine

You are a surviving passenger or crew member of the S.S. *Eastland*. What you experienced that day has changed your life forever.

1 What is your name, occupation, and age?   **2** Why were you on the *Eastland* that day?   **3** What was your mood as you boarded the ship?   **4** What were people wearing?   **5** When did you first sense that something was wrong?   **6** How were you able to survive? **7** What visual image will never leave you?   **8** What sound will you never forget?   **9** Your best friend aboard the ship did not survive the disaster. What happened?   **10** What should be done to memorialize those who died?

The year is 1975. Even though 60 years have passed, the events of July 24, 1915, remain vivid in your memory. Write a letter to the descendants of your best friend, describing your memories of that fateful day.

1916
CARL SANDBURG WRITES "CHICAGO"

Carl Sandburg, 1955. World-Telegram & Sun photograph by Al Ravenna. New York World-Telegram and the Sun Newspaper Photograph Collection (Library of Congress). Available from loc.gov/pictures/item/95517271, accessed August 20, 2013.

Background

The poet Carl Sandburg was one of Chicago's many famous writers. He worked as a journalist, but he also wrote folk songs, biographies of Abraham Lincoln, stories for children, and lots of poetry, some of it extended free verse. "Chicago" is an example of Sandburg's free-verse poetry, and perhaps no poem about the city is better known because Sandburg put into words what people thought of the place—a tough, no nonsense Midwestern city.

Here's how it begins:

Hog Butcher for the World,
Tool Maker, Stacker of Wheat,
Player with Railroads and the Nation's Freight Handler;
Stormy, husky and brawling,
City of the Big Shoulders
They tell me you are wicked and I believe them...

Go online to take a virtual tour of the Carl Sandburg Historic Site Association.

Search online at the Encyclopedia of Chicago on the Chicago History Museum's website to discover more photos, articles, and facts about the writer and his work.

Now that you have familiarized yourself with the poet, write a concise summary of what you have discovered about the man.

Remember

You'll notice that Sandburg talks directly to Chicago. This is a poetic device known as an "apostrophe." It's a way to bring the poet into close contact with the subject and to use a direct, clear, and conversational voice.

Pick a place you know well and for which you have strong feelings.

1 What place have you chosen? 2 Why is it special? 3 Why is it a typical example of such a place? 4 Why is it unique? 5 What would a stranger notice first? 6 What would a stranger not notice? 7 What ordinary objects have special meaning for you? 8 How do others react to this place? 9 How has the place changed? 10 How did this place impact your life?

Consider your answers to these and other thoughts about the place and write a letter to the place itself expressing your honest feelings.

Go Online

Go to **chicago.writethroughamerica.com/csandburg** to access useful links and student writing samples for the Discover and Decide prompts.

Discover

A Carl Sandburg wrote the anthologies *Rootabaga Stories* and a sequel *Rootabaga Pigeons* as an attempt to create Midwestern American fairy tales for his three daughters. Read the tales and write a book review. Then submit your review to the Carl Sandburg Historic Site Association website.

B Using a photo montage of online pictures of both past and contemporary Chicago as a dramatic visual background, organize and perform a Reader's Theater recitation of Sandburg's poem, "Chicago."

C Select some memorable lines from Sandburg's verse, and create a series of posters or T-shirt designs to illustrate them.

D Although he is remembered as the kindly, white-haired biographer of Abraham Lincoln, in his day Carl Sandburg's socialistic and pacifistic views were considered controversial and even radical. Watch the documentary *The Day Carl Sandburg Died* and write a report on the political aspects of Sandburg's work.

Decide

A Thirty-six years before Daniel Day-Lewis's version of Abraham Lincoln hit the theaters, actor Hal Holbrook won an Emmy for "Outstanding Lead Actor in a Limited Series" for his portrayal of the 16th president in *Sandburg's Lincoln*. Watch both films; then write a compare/contrast essay in which you critique the two actors' performances.

B In addition to his other accomplishments, Carl Sandburg collected American folk songs and would often entertain crowds by playing the guitar and singing them. Published in 1927, Sandburg's *The American Songbag* was his attempt to capture the musical voice of America. In his preface to the work, Sandburg pointed out that new musical art forms would soon take their place in the American culture, but he left the task of compiling them to those who would come later. Imagine that you are writing a sequel to Sandburg's book. Compile a list of 10 contemporary songs that you feel should be catalogued in the *21st Century American Songbag,* and write a paragraph for each justifying its inclusion in the anthology.

Imagine

Sandburg uses personification to depict Chicago. For example, we find in the fourth line that Chicago's a human being who is "Stormy, husky and brawling."

Imagine a place that is not like someone who is "stormy, husky and brawling," but instead is…

1 Neat, careful, and annoying. 2 Skinny, sickly, and complaining.
3 Growing, smug, and moving. 4 Graceful, shapely, and fetching.
5 Sly, scowling, and sinister. 6 Silent, sullen, and shadowy.
7 Intelligent, articulate, and challenging. 8 Laughing, taunting, and teasing. 9 Honest, direct, and small. 10 Snarling, threatening, and bullying.

Pick one of these three-word images and describe an imaginary town for which these words would fit. Give the town an appropriate name. Where do the people work? Where do they live? What does the downtown look like? Are there any statues?

AUGUST 3, 1921
WORLD SERIES SCANDAL ROCKS CHICAGO!

Cartoon on the breaking of the Black Sox Scandal. *The Sporting News* (October 7, 1920). Available from Wikimedia Commons file: Eight_men_banned.png, accessed August 20, 2013.

Background

In 1919 the Chicago White Sox won the American League Pennant and played the Cincinnati Reds in the World Series. The Reds won, but it turned out that some of the Sox had conspired with gamblers to throw at least two of the games. For a while it looked like the end of baseball, but Commissioner Kenesaw Mountain Landis took over, and on August 3, 1921, he kicked out eight White Sox players from baseball forever. It was not a happy time in Chicago sports.

Check out the display devoted to Chicago baseball at the *Chicago: Crossroads of America* exhibit at the Chicago History Museum.

Search online at the Encyclopedia of Chicago on the Chicago History Museum's website to discover more photos, articles, and facts about the scandal.

Now write a concise summary of the events of the Black Sox Scandal.

Remember

If you had been around in 1921, you probably would have been bitterly disappointed in what had happened, especially if you were a baseball fan. Recall a time when you were disappointed, when what you hoped to happen did not happen.

1 How old were you when this happened? 2 What was important in your life? 3 What were you looking forward to? 4 Why was this disappointment so particularly meaningful to you? 5 How did the event start? 6 When did you realize things were not going to be as you had hoped? 7 What was the most disappointing moment? 8 How did things end? 9 How did you deal with the disappointment at the time? 10 How do you regard it now?

Write this in the third person as a folktale. Begin with, "Once upon a time there was a person who..."

Go Online

Go to **chicago.writethroughamerica.com/blacksox** to access useful links and student writing samples for the Discover and Decide prompts.

Discover

A Based on W.P. Kinsella's novel *Shoeless Joe,* the film *Field of Dreams* (1989 PG) tells the story of the eight banished White Sox players coming back as spirits to play baseball again in a ballpark nestled in an Iowa corn patch. Take a "virtual" trip to Dyersville, Iowa, and write a report on what you discover.

B Give a speech to your class on the key events of the 1919 Black Sox Scandal. Use either a timeline or a PowerPoint presentation as a visual aid for your speech.

C As an individual project, write a first-person, free-verse poem in the voice of one of the eight banished White Sox.

Or, as a small-group project, write a series of monologues or free-verse poems using the voices of people connected to the Black Sox scandal. Then present the collection as a Reader's Theater event.

D Directed by John Sayles, the movie *Eight Men Out* (1988 PG) is generally considered to be one of the best baseball films ever made. Based on your research, review the film in terms of its historical accuracy.

Decide

A Joe Jackson, one of the banned players, later denied having been part of the conspiracy, but he never returned to baseball. Visit the *Shoeless Joe Jackson Virtual Hall of Fame* website. While there, you can make a suggestion as to what you would like to see kept, removed, or added to the site. Then, using the access provided by the site, write a letter to Major League Baseball Commissioner Bud Selig urging him either to lift or maintain Joe Jackson's listing on the Hall of Fame's "ineligible list."

B Do professional athletes have the responsibility to serve as role models, or is that an inappropriate expectation on the public's part? Write a persuasive essay arguing your position on the question. Use this thesis starter to help focus your argument: "Professional athletes do/do not have an obligation to serve as role models because…"

Imagine

Many others on the Black Sox team did not take any part in the fix, and they continued to play baseball. These men resisted the temptation to take the money.

You are a star athlete. You are approached by a gambler. You are tempted, but you turn the gambler down and do the right thing.

1 What's your name? Your nickname?   2 At what sport do you excel? 3 What are some of your specific achievements?   4 How do the fans treat you?   5 Where are you when the gambler says, "I have an offer to make you"?   6 What financial problems make this seem tempting? 7 What personal problems make this seem tempting?   8 How do you let this person know you will not do it?   9 What happens immediately afterward?   10 How do you follow up on this?

Write this in the first person. Start your story in the middle as the gambler is making the offer. Use a flashback to fill in the background material.

1920
RADICALS SOUND OFF IN BUGHOUSE SQUARE

Washington Square Park, Chicago. From *Chicago's Parks* by John Graf (Arcadia Publishing, 2000, p. 97). Available from Wikimedia Commons file: Bughouse_Square.jpg, accessed August 25, 2013.

Background

In a small park on the Near North Side of Chicago, across Walton Street from the Newberry Library, is a spot where in the 1920s and 1930s people poured in to listen to and often heckle public speakers ranting about controversial subjects. The subjects of these speeches were usually political and almost always highly radical. The actual name of the park is Washington Square Park. It was given the "bughouse" nickname because the term was once slang for a mental institution. Bughouse Square is still there and people do occasionally show up to shoot off their mouths, but it is not like the old days when this small park was once considered the "center of free speech in America."

Check out information on Bughouse Square at the Newberry Library.

Search online at the Encyclopedia of Chicago at the Chicago History Museum's website to discover more photos, articles, and facts about Bughouse Square and the people who spoke there.

Now write a concise summary of the history of this colorful site.

Remember

Ask a parent, another relative, a teacher, or someone else of an older generation to describe a speech that moved him or her. The speech could have been heard live or on television.

Ask your subject:

1 Where were your at the time that you heard the speech?   2 Why was the speech being given?   3 What qualified the speaker to give the speech?   4 What was the subject of the speech?   5 What was the speaker's approach?   6 How did the speaker keep your attention? 7 What particular lines do you remember?   8 How did you react immediately afterward?   9 What effect did it have later on?   10 How do you think the speech would be regarded today?

Write this up as a question and answer piece. Add any other questions that might be necessary.

Go Online

Go to **chicago.writethroughamerica.com/bughouse** to access useful links and student writing samples for the Discover and Decide prompts.

Discover

A One of the most controversial and tireless advocates for social reform in Chicago history was Lucy Parsons, a likely former slave who moved with her husband to Chicago in 1873 and fought for various causes until her death in 1942. Learn about this remarkable social activist who spoke at Bughouse Square, and create a timeline of the events of her life.

B Many of the most animated speakers at Bughouse Square were members of the Industrial Workers of the World (IWW) or "Wobblies." Research the IWW and give a speech on its history.

C One of the most colorful venues for free speech in Chicago was the Dill Pickle Club. Marked by a sign at the door that urged patrons to "step high, stoop low, leave your dignity outside," the club was a haven for freethinkers of all kinds. As a small group project, write and perform a one-act play set in the Dill Pickle Club. Begin your play with a naive visitor to Chicago wandering into the club by mistake.

D In 2010, the Newberry Library presented its Altgeld Freedom of Speech Award to Kartemquin Films for its 45 years of producing documentary films "that examine and critique society through the stories of real people." Watch a Kartemquin film, write a review, and submit the review to your school or local newspaper.

Decide

A Write a letter to the mayor of Chicago in which you propose 10 specific suggestions for improving the city. Rank the list from least important to most important, and write a short paragraph clarifying/justifying each proposed improvement.

B Select a personal issue that many people would not consider to be particularly important but matters to you. Then write an essay arguing your position, using this thesis starter: "Although some people might consider this issue to be rather silly, the world would be a better place if..." Incorporate quotes from peers, relatives, and teachers to support your position.

Imagine

Imagine that you are in the crowd at a place like Bughouse Square. The speakers have been noisy. You've enjoyed shouting back at them. One of the speeches that really gets your attention calls for the abolishment of one of the following:

1 Money   2 Team sports   3 Dessert   4 Vacations   5 Jewelry
6 Busses   7 Comic books   8 Gossip   9 Whispering   10 Pets

Pick one of these and write the speech. Make it ridiculous but logical in its own way. Then describe what happens when the speaker delivers the speech. Make sure you set the scene. Don't forget the hecklers.

1924
"MAN-EATERS OF TSAVO" COME TO CHICAGO

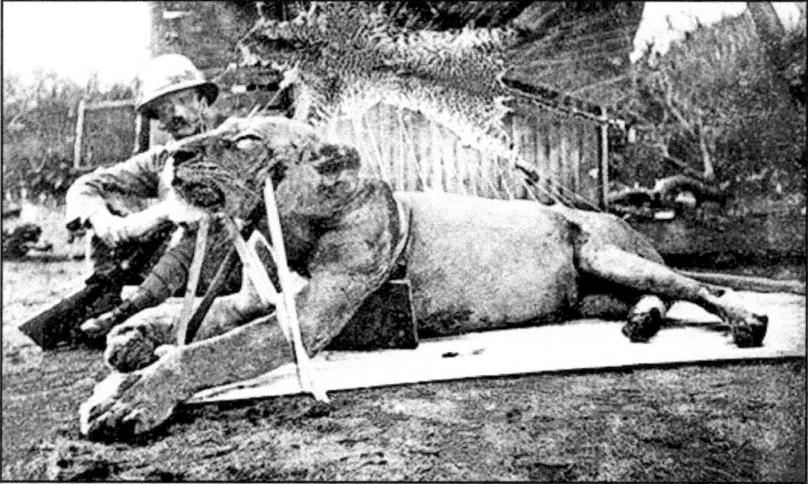

The first of the two Tsavo man-eating lions shot by Lt. Colonel Patterson, 1898. Available from smithsonianmag.com/science-nature/Man-Eaters-of-Tsavo.html, accessed August 25, 2013.

Background

The Field Museum is one of Chicago's great treasures. It is hard to imagine visiting our city and not going to this museum. And, of course, we go there not to find out what happened here in Chicago but what happened somewhere far away. Museums bring the world to us. After speaking at The Field Museum in 1924 about his experiences in Africa hunting man-eating lions, explorer and author John Henry Patterson sold the museum the lion skins and skulls for the then-sizeable sum of $5,000. This purchase of the hides of killer lions is a good example of the kind of acquisitions a museum can make and how much these artifacts can expand our world.

Check out the display devoted to the lions of Tsavo at the Chicago Field Museum of Natural History.

Search online at The Chicago Field Museum of Natural History's website to discover more articles about the man-eaters of Tsavo.

Now write a concise summary of the story of the man-eaters of Tsavo.

Remember

Write a true animal story, maybe one that took place in Chicago. This could be about a pet—yours or someone else's—or about an animal you read or heard about in the news. You can make it funny or sad, but be sure to make it memorable. It's something you want to share—a good story.

1 What kind of animal was it? If a pet, whose pet?   2 What was this animal's usual behavior?   3 What happened that was so unusual?
4 If you were there, how did you react?   5 How did others react?
6 Was this a cause for alarm?   7 How long did the animal continue this unusual behavior?   8 How was it finally resolved?   9 Did this change your feelings about the animal?   10 What did this prove to you about animals in general or this animal in particular?

Write this as a story intended for a young audience.

Go Online

Go to **chicago.writethroughamerica.com/maneaters** to access useful links and student writing samples for the Discover and Decide prompts.

Discover

A Though the Tsavo lions are famous, they are probably not as closely associated with the city of Chicago as their bronze counterparts outside the Art Institute. Write an article on the history of these two sculptures. Be sure to include the various seasonal "outfits" they sport throughout the year.

B A number of theories have been proposed regarding why the Tsavo lions became man-eaters. Learn more about the subject; then share your findings in a speech or video documentary.

C The Field Museum is one of three museums that share a "campus" on the Chicago lakefront: the Field Museum, the Adler Planetarium, and the Shedd Aquarium. Investigate all three, and then create three posters—one for each museum, promoting a particular attraction the museum offers to the public.

D Visit the lions at either the Lincoln Park Zoo or the Brookfield Zoo. Take your camera along and create a photo essay on the experience to share with your class.

Decide

A Although two major motion pictures, *The Ghost and the Darkness* (1996 R) and *Bwana Devil* (1952 NR), have been based on the Tsavo lions, the films take rather different approaches to the subject. Based on your research, review the two movie versions and assess the accuracy of their depictions of the hunt for the Tsavo lions.

B The population of wild lions in Africa is becoming increasingly endangered, but controversy surrounds efforts to protect these vanishing animals. Research the options; then write a newspaper editorial presenting your opinion on how to deal best with the situation. Give it a title.

Imagine

What you read about these lions and what you imagine when you see their hides should give you some ideas for a good old-fashioned adventure story. Try writing something from a lion's point of view, as the leader of the pack.

1 What do your fellow lions call you? How did you earn that nickname?   **2** As the leader of the pride, what are your duties? How do you keep control?   **3** What threat do human beings suddenly pose? **4** What would happen if nothing were done about this?   **5** Why are these humans particularly dangerous?   **6** What do the young lions recommend as the best solutions?   **7** What do the older, more cautious lions recommend?   **8** What does your best friend recommend? **9** How do you finally solve this human problem?   **10** What has this experience taught you about solving problems?

Give this a good title. Begin with, "Once upon a time…"

1929
ELIOT NESS TAKES ON AL CAPONE

Eliot Ness, *c.* 1933. Available from Wikimedia Commons file: Eliotness.jpg, accessed August 25, 2013.

Background

In 1929 Federal Prohibition Agent and Chicago native Eliot Ness was assigned the job of heading a special team to bring down notorious gangster Al Capone—who had been doing pretty much whatever he wanted. His gang had most certainly been responsible for the St. Valentine's Day Massacre, yet he was never arrested for it.

Ness and his team of prohibition agents closed down places where alcohol was made and places where it was sold. His efforts led to the destruction of Capone's million-dollar brewery business and made life more difficult for the gangster, but in the end Capone was brought down for failure to pay his income tax.

After Chicago, Ness moved on to Cleveland, where he continued to fight crime. Through the years Ness's name has lived on as the person who stood up to Capone. Many films and TV shows have kept that reputation alive.

Check out the display on Al Capone and Chicago crime at the *Chicago: Crossroads of America* exhibit at the Chicago History Museum.

Search online at the Encyclopedia of Chicago on the Chicago History Museum's website to discover more photos, articles, and facts about Ness and his team, the Untouchables.

Now that you have familiarized yourself with Eliot Ness and the Untouchables, write a concise summary of his battle with organized crime in Chicago.

Remember

Gangsters like Al Capone are bullies. They use whatever force is necessary to get what they want and take great pleasure in knowing that people fear them. However, bullies don't have to be tolerated. Most of us have memories of times when someone successfully stood up to a bully. Ask 10 people to recall a time that they saw a bully get what he or she deserved. Write a short summary of each anecdote.

How should people deal with bullies? Think of a time you saw or heard about someone dealing effectively with a bully. Here are some possible candidates:

1 Parent 2 Teacher 3 Coach 4 Artist 5 Religious figure
6 Friend 7 Police officer 8 Soldier 9 Teacher 10 Security guard

Pick the one you like best and expand it into a full narrative with a distinct beginning, middle, and ending.

Go Online

Go to **chicago.writethroughamerica.com/eness** to access useful links and student writing samples for the Discover and Decide prompts.

Discover

A One of the most anticlimactic moments in television history was the much-hyped opening of Al Capone's "secret" vault by investigative reporter Geraldo Rivera on April 21, 1986. Write a report on the infamous documentary special that ironically launched the national career of Rivera.

B Although no one was ever convicted of any involvement with the St. Valentine's Day Massacre, it is generally accepted that Al Capone's gang was responsible for the slayings. Give a speech on this infamous moment in Chicago history.

C The British writers of the '70s hit song "The Night Chicago Died" admitted that they knew very little about Chicago or its history. Listen to the song. Then write a better version of its lyrics based on your research.

D Al Capone was not the only "Public Enemy Number One" with a Chicago connection. On July 22, 1934, notorious bank robber John Dillinger was shot and killed by Chicago policemen and federal agents outside the Biograph Theater on Lincoln Avenue. Take your camera to the site and create a PowerPoint presentation on the shooting. You may want to watch *Manhattan Melodrama,* the movie Dillinger and the notorious "Lady in Red" viewed at the Biograph just before he was killed.

Decide

A Watch either the film *The Untouchables* (1987 R) starring Kevin Costner as Eliot Ness or an episode of *The Untouchables* television series starring Robert Stack. Based on your research, write a review on the accuracy of the depiction of Ness and his team.

B Although the Roaring Twenties ended more than 90 years ago, many people still immediately identify Chicago with the days of gangsters and speakeasies. Research the era and write an essay using this thesis starter: "The world seems fascinated with Chicago's 1920s image because…"

Imagine

Imagine that by accident you pay a visit to a place totally controlled by the mob. At first it feels quite normal, but after a few hours there, you know for certain that this peaceful little place is not what it seems.

1 What do you overhear people saying while you are waiting for a cab?   2 What does the cabdriver tell you?   3 What's the headline of the local newspaper?   4 What's a smaller story on page four?   5 How does the doorman treat you at the hotel?   6 In the lobby two men are arguing. What are they saying to each other?   7 In your hotel room, you find a note in the desk. What does it say?   8 You turn on the TV. What has just happened?   9 You decide to leave. What does the desk clerk do?   10 How does the cop on the street treat you as you wait for a cab?

Later, on a bus out of town, you write a letter to the FBI. Add as many vivid details as you would like.

AUGUST 15, 1930
ORPHAN GORILLA ARRIVES AT LINCOLN PARK ZOO

Bushman at Lincoln Park Zoo (1947). Chicago History Museum. Image cropped and brightened.

Background

Bushman the gorilla was a big deal—a 500-pound big deal. An orphaned infant gorilla, he was brought to Chicago on August 15, 1930, by the directors of the Lincoln Park Zoo. Just a 38-pound two-year-old when he arrived, Bushman grew and grew and quickly became a city celebrity. He eventually reached 547 pounds. The nation's zoo directors voted him "the most outstanding animal in any zoo in the world."

Over the years, millions of people came to see Bushman. He was usually in a good mood, but sometimes he would throw his food (or worse) at people. He made the news when he briefly escaped in 1950. He wandered around for a while and then, scared by a snake, returned to his cage on his own. Mourners passed by his cage for weeks after he died on New Year's Day 1951. His remains are at the Field Museum.

Check out the display devoted to Bushman at the Chicago Field Museum.

Search online at the Encyclopedia of Chicago on the Chicago History Museum's website to discover more information about the Lincoln Park Zoo.

Now write a concise summary of what you have learned about this remarkable primate.

Remember

Describe a typical visit you made to the zoo when you were little. How did it start? How did it end? Here are some things to think about:

1 Getting there   2 Entering the zoo   3 The first animals you saw
4 Elephants and other really big animals   5 Lions   6 Snakes and other reptiles   7 Sounds   8 Other visitors   9 Children's area
10 Leaving the zoo

Write an account of your day at the zoo. Use plenty of sensory details to make the day come alive for your readers. Describe your feelings.

Go Online

Go to **chicago.writethroughamerica.com/bushman** to access useful links and student writing samples for the Discover and Decide prompts.

Discover

A The founding of Lincoln Park Zoo in 1868 may seem like a long time ago, but archaeologists have found evidence of early zoos dating back thousands of years. Learn more about the history of zoos, and write a one-page report on the origin and evolution of these institutions.

B Although the Chicago area has the unique advantage of having two world-class zoos, each is unique in concept, philosophy, and design. Visit both zoos' websites and discover what each zoo has to offer. Then with a partner or panel of classmates, conduct a debate over which zoo—Brookfield or Lincoln Park—would be the better choice for a class trip.

C In 1947, one writer described Bushman's presence as *"a nightmare that escaped from darkness into daylight and has exchanged its insubstantial form for 550 pounds of solid flesh. His face is one that might be expected to gloat through the troubled dreams that follow overindulgence. His hand is the kind of thing a sleeper sees reaching for him just before he wakes up screaming."* Incorporating the words from this description, write a combination found/original free-verse poem about Bushman.

D Take a notebook and camera to record your observations during a trip to the Lincoln Park Zoo. Afterward submit your zoo story and photographs to the *Lincoln Park Zoo Magazine* website.

Decide

A Some animal-rights activists argue that keeping wild animals in captivity is ethically wrong. Others maintain that zoos provide security and contribute to wildlife conservation. Investigate the issue and form your own opinion. Then write a newspaper editorial arguing either for or against the existence of zoos.

B Although thousands of animals have resided at the Lincoln Park Zoo since its opening in 1868, no other animal has had an impact on Chicagoans like Bushman. Research the Bushman phenomenon, and write an essay explaining the reasons why this particular animal had such a fan following.

Imagine

Pretend that you are a zoo animal (you can decide which one). You are the biggest attraction of all. You like being the center of attention, but you don't always like the people. You've got a bit of an attitude. What's a typical day like for you? After you introduce yourself, make sure you talk about…

1 The person who feeds you. **2** Other people who work at the zoo.
3 The contact you have with other animals. **4** Likable children.
5 Not-so likable children. **6** Old people. **7** People with cameras.
8 Eccentric people. **9** Your favorite visitor. **10** Your favorite time of the day.

Write this as a rant to the animals in nearby cages.

MAY 17, 1943
WRIGLEY STARTS WOMEN'S BASEBALL LEAGUE

Fort Wayne Daisies player, Marie Wegman, of the All American Girls Professional League arguing with umpire Norris Ward—Opa-loka, Florida, 1948. State Archives of Florida, *Florida Memory*, floridamemory.com/items/show/56235, accessed August 25, 2013.

Background

Like all American cities, Chicago was deeply involved in World War II. Soldiers from our city fought in battles all over the world. Many were trained at Fort Sheridan and other nearby bases. Our factories manufactured war material. But while Chicagoans had a lot to do, they also needed entertainment—like baseball. And with so many men in the service, why not have a league for women? P.K. Wrigley, the owner of the Chicago Cubs, thought this would be a good idea. On May 17, 1943, spring training began at Wrigley Field for the All-American Girls Softball League, as the league was known at first.

Search online at the Illinois Periodicals Online Project (IPO) on the Northern Illinois University website to access photos and facts on women's baseball.

Search online at the Encyclopedia of Chicago on the Chicago History Museum's website to discover more about the All-American Girls Baseball League.

Now that you have familiarized yourself with the subject, write a concise summary of the history of women's professional baseball in Chicago.

Remember

Think of all the groups to which you've belonged—your family, your class at school, a club, a team, and so on. Recall a time when group morale was low, nothing was working, and people were complaining.

1 What was the group? When did this happen? 2 How was the group supposed to function? 3 What was one of the signs that things were not going well? 4 What was another indication? 5 How did people start to deal with the group's low morale? 6 How well did the solution work? 7 What else did people try? 8 How well did the alternatives work? 9 Was the problem finally solved? 10 What did you learn from all of this?

Write this as a news article with a headline, lead paragraph, and supporting details.

Go Online

Go to **chicago.writethroughamerica.com/wleague** to access useful links and student writing samples for the Discover and Decide prompts.

Discover

A Watch the film *A League of Their Own* (1992 PG), a fictionalized account of the early days of women's professional baseball. Based on your research, write a review examining the historical accuracy of the film.

B Professional baseball was only one of several formerly all-male occupations filled by women during World War II. Research the role of women on the WWII home front. Narrow your focus to an aspect you find interesting, and create a PowerPoint presentation or video documentary of your findings.

C While competing on a barnstorming baseball tour in 1931, New York Yankee immortals Babe Ruth and Lou Gehrig were both struck out by Jackie Mitchell, a 17-year-old female pitcher for the Class AA Chattanooga Lookouts. Learn more about this memorable story. Then write a scene portraying the event for a movie script about the life of Jackie Mitchell.

D The number of women still alive who played in the All-American Girls Professional Baseball League decreases each year. Go to the league's website to access information about an individual player. Perhaps you can even contact a surviving veteran of the league. Present your findings to the class.

Decide

A Do you think women will ever break the "gender barrier" in professional baseball, football, or basketball? Research the subject and write an essay using the following thesis starter: "It is likely/unlikely that women will eventually integrate into men's major professional sports because…"

B Despite the steadily increasing involvement of women in competitive sports, women's sports continue to lack the media coverage and audience of men's sports. Write an opinion piece for a magazine arguing that the popularity of women's sports will/will not eventually catch up with men's sports.

Imagine

Imagine that you are selected to play on the first all-girls professional base-ball team. Your first game proves to be extremely challenging, but ultimately a great success.

1 How old are you? What else do you like besides baseball?   2 How did you find out about the girls' team? Did you have any doubts?
3 Why were you so impressive at the tryouts?   4 When you took the field, what were some of the rude reactions from the crowd?   5 How did you respond to these?   6 What were some of the positive crowd reactions?   7 Why was this game so exciting?   8 Why were you the star?   9 How did your teammates respond?   10 What did the crowd do?

After the game you write a personal narrative in your journal. The title of the narrative is "I Did It!"

SEPTEMBER 27, 1950
GWENDOLYN BROOKS WINS PULITZER PRIZE

Gwendolyn Brooks. MDCarchives. Available from Wikimedia Commons file: Gwendolynbrooks.jpg, accessed August 20, 2013.

Background

Chicago is known for its great writers, not just its gangsters and tall buildings. Of the many famous writers who were based in Chicago, few are as well known as Gwendolyn Brooks. Her "We Real Cool" is one of the most anthologized poems in American literature. And as an African American writer, she can take credit for knocking down racial barriers. Her second book of poetry, *Annie Allen,* was awarded the Pulitzer Prize on September 27, 1950, making Brooks the first African American to receive the Pulitzer for poetry. The subjects of her poems and her style make us aware of life for African Americans in Chicago and elsewhere.

Check out information on Gwendolyn Brooks at the DuSable Museum of African American History.

Visit the Poetry Foundation at 61 West Superior Street or go online at the Foundation's website to learn more about Gwendolyn Brooks and her writing career.

Now that you have familiarized yourself with Gwendolyn Brooks, write a concise summary of what you have learned about the poet and her work.

Remember

"We Real Cool" is about people who don't realize that what they do now will matter later on. Recall a time when you made a decision (maybe not willingly) that you believed would make things better for you in the future. This could be a school decision, a health decision, a family decision, or anything else that really mattered.

1 How old were you at the time? What was important in your life?
2 Who were the most important influences in your life?   3 What difficult choice did you have to make?   4 Why would it have been more pleasant to avoid this choice?   5 Whom would you have disappointed if you had taken the easy way out?   6 Did you come up with any safer choices you could have made?   7 Why did you finally do the right thing?   8 What were the immediate results?   9 How did things work out later on?   10 What did you learn from this?

Write a diary entry congratulating yourself for your wise choice.

Go Online

Go to **chicago.writethroughamerica.com/gbrooks** to access useful links and student writing samples for the Discover and Decide prompts.

Discover

A Read some of Gwendolyn Brooks's poetry. Then respond in an informal journal entry to the three poems that impact you the most.

B Select three of Gwendolyn Brooks's poems and perform them for your class, either individually or in a small group presentation.

C Select a particularly striking image from a Gwendolyn Brooks poem, and design a poster or T-shirt to illustrate it.

D Attend a poetry slam and write a review. Submit the review to either your local or high school newspaper, or post it on a blog.

Decide

A Young Chicago Authors, a Chicago youth program, sponsors "Louder Than a Bomb," an annual city-wide teen poetry slam competition. Write a letter to your favorite English teacher, urging that person to sponsor a LTAB poetry team at your school.

B In the film *Dead Poet's Society* (1989 PG), English teacher John Keating attempts to explain to his class his passion for poetry: "*We don't read and write poetry because it's cute. We read and write poetry because we are members of the human race. And the human race is filled with passion. And medicine, law, business, engineering, these are noble pursuits and necessary to sustain life. But poetry, beauty, romance, love, these are what we stay alive for.*"

Write a letter to someone for whom poetry has no appeal. Use excerpts from favorite poems to help illustrate your argument that poetry truly matters.

Imagine

Read "We Real Cool" (below). Now, pick another group of people who, like the characters in this poem, consider themselves, in an utterly unrealistic way, to be super cool. These could be high-school students, business people, or any other group of people who seem overly pleased with their reputation.

1 Who are these people?   2 How do you happen to know them? Have you had personal contact with them?   3 How do they dress? 4 What can you say about their body language?   5 How do they talk? What are some of their favorite expressions?   6 How are they viewed by other people?   7 What kind of work do they do or will they do? 8 What can you say about their future?   9 What could lead them to change their lifestyles?   10 What will happen if they keep acting the way they do?

Using the form of "We Real Cool" write a poem about the "cool" people you have identified. Here's the poem:

WE REAL COOL

The Pool Players.
Seven at the Golden Shovel.

We real cool. We
Left school. We

Lurk late. We
Strike straight. We

Sing sin. We
Thin gin. We

Jazz June. We
Die soon.

APRIL 15, 1955
FIRST MCDONALD'S FRANCHISE OPENS

McDonald's store #1 located west of Chicago, Illinois. Photograph by Carol M. Highsmith (Library of Congress). Available from loc.gov/pictures/item/2011631143, accessed August 25, 2013.

Background

In 1954, Ray Kroc, an Oak Park salesman who sold milk-shake machines, convinced the McDonald brothers of San Bernardino, California, to make him the sole franchising agent of their hamburger stand. On April 15 of the next year, Kroc opened a restaurant in Des Plaines, Illinois, and the rest is fast-food history. While it was not the first fast-food restaurant, McDonald's became the biggest. Today there are more than 33,000 McDonald's restaurants in at least 119 countries serving more than 68 million customers every day. More than 400,000 people work for McDonald's, including approximately 6,000 in Chicago alone.

Check out the re-creation of the original McDonald's restaurant at the McDonald's #1 Store Museum in Des Plaines, Illinois.

Take a tour of McDonald's Hamburger University at 2715 Jorie Boulevard, Oak Brook, Illinois, to discover first hand more about this fast-food giant.

Now that you have familiarized yourself with the history of McDonald's, write a concise summary of what you have discovered.

Remember

People who write about the significance of places like McDonald's are writing about popular culture—the features of our culture that most of us share. How typical of your peer group are your particular tastes and habits? What is your taste in...

1 Movies?   2 Books?   3 Magazines?   4 Casual clothes?   5 Dressy clothes?   6 Speaking style?   7 Hobbies?   8 Television shows?   9 Music?   10 Art?

Put these responses together into a description of yourself from a third-person point of view, as if you were describing someone else.

Go Online

Go to **chicago.writethroughamerica.com/mcdonalds** to access useful links and student writing samples for the Discover and Decide prompts.

Discover

A McDonald's has changed quite a bit over the years. Research the history of the company, and create a list of the 10 most significant changes that have occurred since 1955.

B Although McDonald's has been serving up hamburgers since 1955, the origin of the hamburger itself may be traced as far back as the 1300s or even earlier. Research the history of the hamburger and create a PowerPoint presentation or present an informative speech on the historical high points of this ubiquitous taste treat.

C A surprising number of songs have been written over the years about hamburgers. Check out a few of them online; then write your own song or rap about America's favorite sandwich.

D How does McDonald's compare to other fast-food franchises in terms of cost, nutrition, popularity, etc.? Learn more about McDonald's' rivals, and create some graphs and charts comparing five significant aspects of these fast-food chains. You may wish to do a little firsthand research of your own, and sample their offerings for yourself!

Decide

A Under pressure from various health and children's advocacy organizations, McDonald's has recently adjusted its Happy Meals menu. Research the changes made, and then grade McDonald's on its role in promoting or combating childhood obesity in America.

B Over the years McDonald's has expanded from that first restaurant in Des Plaines to more than 33,000 restaurants in 119 countries. This expansion, however, has not always been successful. Read about McDonald's' international expansion. Then write an essay analyzing what it is about this fast-food franchise that makes it work in some countries but not in others.

Imagine

The year is 1955. You are a teenager cruising Rand Road in your father's 1952 Studebaker with Elvis's latest song playing on the radio. You are going to check out this new joint called "McDonald's" that your friends have been telling you so much about.

1 What is your name? How old are you? Where do you go to high school?   2 What kind of music do you like best?   3 What are you wearing?   4 Who is in the car with you?   5 What have your friends told you about McDonald's?   6 Where are you going after you leave McDonald's?   7 What do you first notice as you enter the restaurant? 8 What are three smells that you can identify?   9 What unexpected thing happens in the restaurant?   10 What do you order? Do you enjoy your meal? Will you return again?

Write a short story in which you recount this first experience at McDonald's. Use the restaurant as the setting for your narrative, but focus on the unexpected event that occurs there. Be sure to get across your teenager's personality through the voice of the narrator.

JULY 1955
CHESS BROTHERS RELEASE "MAYBELLENE"

Chuck Berry. Universal Attractions (management). Available from Wikimedia Commons file: Chuck_Berry_1971.jpg, accessed August 25, 2013.

Background

Leonard and Phil Chess, co-owners of the Chicago-based record label Chess Records, were pioneers in the early days of rock 'n' roll music. In a time when many record companies shied away from recording African American artists, Chess Records signed Bo Diddley, Willie Dixon, Muddy Waters, Howlin' Wolf, Etta James, and many others. In July 1955, "Maybellene" was Chuck Berry's first release on the Chess label. The song went to number five on the pop chart and held the number one position on the *Billboard R&B* chart for 11 weeks.

The Chess brothers' decision to give black musicians a chance led to Chicago becoming one of the great music towns in the country.

Check out Willie Dixon's Blues Heaven Foundation Museum at 2120 South Michigan Avenue, the site of the original Chess Records studios.

Search online at the Encyclopedia of Chicago on the Chicago History Museum's website to discover more articles and facts about Chess Records.

Now that you have familiarized yourself with the history of Chess Records, write a concise summary of what you have discovered about the early days of Chicago rock 'n' roll.

Remember

The Chess brothers were savvy promoters. But they and others who followed them were also risk takers, challenging people who felt the races should not be together. Write about a time when you took an unpopular stand.

1 How old were you at the time? What things were important to you? 2 Why did you feel the need to take a stand? 3 What was the issue? What were your choices? What did you choose? 4 Why was your decision so courageous? What did you have to lose if you were not successful? 5 What was the immediate result of your taking a stand? 6 How did events develop afterward? 7 Were there any moments when you considered abandoning your position? 8 How did this episode finally end? 9 How was your life changed because of the stand that you took? 10 When you look back, would you have done anything differently?

Write this story as an internal argument between the part of you who wants to do the right thing and the part who wants to do the safe thing.

Go Online

Go to **chicago.writethroughamerica.com/chessbro** to access useful links and student writing samples for the Discover and Decide prompts.

Discover

A Do all generations object to the next generation's music? How similar is the current controversy over "objectionable" or "explicit" lyrics in rap music to the public reaction to early rock 'n' roll? Make a Venn diagram showing both the similarities and differences of the two conflicts.

B In 1987, Leonard Chess was inducted into the Rock and Roll Hall of Fame in Cleveland. Go to the Hall of Fame's website to learn more about the Chess legacy. Then design a PowerPoint presentation that highlights their contributions. Be sure to add some selections from Chess artists to use as background music.

C Design a poster (individual project) or mural (small group project) that commemorates the history of the Chicago blues scene.

D Do you know anyone who has strong memories of Chicago in the 1950s? Interview that person. What does this person remember about the Chicago music scene at the time? What concerts or rock 'n' roll shows did this person attend? What were they like?

Decide

A In order to make early rock 'n' roll songs more "acceptable" to mainstream white audiences, many 1950s white musicians rerecorded or "covered" songs originally written and recorded by black artists. Did this practice furnish black musicians with opportunities or was it an exploitation of their talents? Go online to hear both original and cover versions of these early rock classics. Then read more about this practice in the music industry.

Write an essay arguing your choice, beginning with this thesis starter: "The practice of white artists in the 1950s covering black artists' material was/ was not exploitative because…"

B In 2008, Chess Records was the subject of two different films: *Cadillac Records* (R) and *Who Do You Love?* (NR). Watch both films, and write a review that argues that one film is the more accurate version of the Chess Records story.

Imagine

Some people have talent and some do not. Of those who don't have talent, some can spot talent in others. And, a few, like the Chess brothers, know how to help the talented person reach a wider audience. Imagine you are a high school kid who's really good at helping others discover and use their talents. Briefly explain how you help each of the following people. Each presents a challenge, but like the Chess brothers you figure out a way to help them share their talents.

1 Jody, a hopelessly shy drummer   2 Rex, a guitarist who knows only Bulgarian rap   3 Stella, a beautiful singer with a ridiculously soft voice   4 Babs, an artist who deeply resents sharing her portraits of famous people   5 Basil, a performer who has no time to work on his tap dancing   6 Wanda, a temperamental glassblower   7 Felix, a writer of overly long poems   8 Mildred, an author whose children's stories once received bad reviews   9 Ferdy, a controversial performance poet   10 Pedro, a self-taught ventriloquist

Pick the one that you would like to develop and tell the whole story. Concentrate on how you help the artist overcome the problem and then how you find the right place for his or her work to be shared.

DECEMBER 1, 1958
95 DIE IN SCHOOL FIRE!

Firemen in the aftermath of Our Lady of Angels Fire, 1958. Negative no. 50772. Photograph by Chicago Daily News, Inc. Chicago History Museum. Image cropped.

Background

Shortly before classes were to be dismissed on the afternoon of December 1, 1958, a small fire that had started in a cardboard trash barrel in the basement spread rapidly through the halls of Our Lady of the Angels School, a parish school in the Humboldt Park neighborhood. Hundreds of students and teachers crawled through smoke-infested hallways and staircases while others jumped from second-floor windows to the frozen ground 25 feet below. Although firemen were able to rescue some 160 students from the roaring inferno, 92 children and three nuns lost their lives as a result of the fire.

For more background information on the Our Lady of the Angels fire:

Check out the display devoted to the Our Lady of the Angels fire at the Fire Museum of Greater Chicago at 5218 South Western Avenue.

Search online at the Encyclopedia of Chicago at the Chicago History Museum's website to discover articles and facts about the tragedy.

Now that you have familiarized yourself with the event, write a concise summary of the day's tragic fire.

Remember

People tend to remember exactly where they were when they first heard the news of a public tragedy, such as the attacks on the World Trade Center in 2001, or a private grief, such as the death of a loved one. Choose one such moment.

1 What was the tragic event? How did you first hear about it?
2 How old were you at the time? What was important to you at the time?   3 Why did you consider this event so significant?   4 What was your first reaction?   5 How did your reaction compare with others' reactions?   6 Did your reaction stay the same, or did you react differently as time went on?   7 Did the event change your life in any permanent way?   8 Did you have private thoughts that you didn't share?   9 What images will stand out in your memory?   10 At the time, what did this prove to you?

Write a letter to yourself to be opened 20 years from now about your reactions to this public or private traumatic moment in your life.

Go Online

Go to **chicago.writethroughamerica.com/olafire** to access useful links and student writing samples for the Discover and Decide prompts.

Discover

A In 2005 Francis Cardinal George invited Fr. Bob Lombardo, a Franciscan priest, to begin a project at the site of Our Lady of the Angels. Learn what is going on at the site. Then write a 500-word newspaper article about Fr. Lombardo's work.

B Interview an administrator at your school. What precautions have been enacted to insure public safety in case of fire or other disasters? Share your findings in a PowerPoint presentation to your class.

C Michael Mason, a survivor of the fire and now a firefighter and paramedic in Downers Grove, Illinois, has compiled a CD of music dedicated to his fallen classmates and teachers from Our Lady of the Angels. Research the events of December 1, 1958. Then compile your own list of 10 songs that could serve as a soundtrack to a documentary examining the tragedy.

D The Our Lady of the Angels website contains a detailed list of many of the people who attempted to help the victims of the fire. Search online for more information on these unsung heroes and write a tribute to one you find remarkable.

Decide

A How should the legacy of the Our Lady of the Angels fire best be commemorated? Write a proposal describing an appropriate memorial for the victims and survivors of this tragic occurrence. Viewing photographs online will help you to visualize the tragedy. Send your proposal to the Commission on Chicago Landmarks.

B The Our Lady of the Angels School had passed a routine fire inspection just weeks before the tragedy of December 1, 1958. Research the changes in fire safety in Chicago in the years since the Our Lady of the Angels fire. Then write an essay answering the question: Has enough been done to insure that such an event cannot happen again?

Imagine

The nuns teaching at Our Lady of the Angels School on that horrific December day were truly heroic, risking their lives to save their students. Without their selfless courage, many more children might have died. Can you think of other people who might become heroes in unexpected ways? Look at this list of people below, and in a sentence or two, explain how certain circumstances could turn each into a hero.

1 Librarian   2 Babysitter   3 Bus driver   4 Football coach
5 Crossing guard   6 Grandmother   7 Gardener   8 Actor
9 Cabdriver   10 Artist

Choose the situation where you can imagine a hero emerging the most clearly, and write it up as a story with a beginning, middle, and end.

JUNE 20, 1960
BOZO PREMIERS ON WGN

Photo postcard of Oliver O. Oliver, Bozo the Clown, Sandy the Clown, and Ringmaster Ned on Bozo's Circus, *c*. 1961. WGN-TV. Available from Wikimedia Commons file: Bozos_Circus_postcard_1960s. jpg, accessed August 25, 2013.

Background

Bozo the Clown, one of the most popular of all children's television charac-ters, did not originate in Chicago. The Chicago franchise of the show, how-ever, was the most widely watched because it appeared on WGN, a cable Su-perstation that eventually broadcast the show all over the country. It started airing in Chicago at noon on June 20, 1960, and it continued in one form or another until 2001. Children loved *Bozo's Circus*. According to the PBS se-ries, *Pioneers of Television*, it was "the most popular and successful locally produced children's program in the history of television." Adults might have been concerned with politics, sports, and crime, but the kids were watching a clown with red hair.

Check out the display devoted to "Early Chicago Television" at the *Chicago: Crossroads of America* exhibit at the Chicago History Museum.

Search online at the Encyclopedia of Chicago on the Chicago History Museum's website to discover articles and facts about Bozo.

Now write a concise summary of the career of Chicago's favorite clown.

Remember

Who was your favorite TV character when you were small? Was it Bozo or someone else? Write down what you recall about this figure.

1 What was the name of the character? Was this a good name?
2 What was the name of the show? What was the character's role on the show?   3 What did the character look like?   4 What did the character sound like?   5 What were some of the typical situations the character was caught in?   6 How did the character make you laugh?   7 What else did the character make you feel?   8 Describe some typical behavior of this character.   9 What was something this character would not do?   10 When did this character start being less interesting for you?

Write a reflective piece explaining why this character meant so much to you.

Go Online

Go to **chicago.writethroughamerica.com/bozo** to access useful links and student writing samples for the Discover and Decide prompts.

Discover

A At the time that Jim Henson and his Muppets were first gathering national attention, Chicago puppeteer Bill Jackson was making a name for himself on the local scene. Research Bill Jackson's work, and write a report on this man's contributions to Chicago television.

B One of the highlights of *Bozo's Circus* was the Grand Prize Game, which can be easily re-created using a board (optional), six buckets, and a ping-pong ball. Deliver a speech on WGN's longest-running program, and invite a member of your own "studio audience" to participate in this test of skill.

C As a small group project, write a pilot scene for a proposed children's television program (see Imagine). Then present it to your class in either a live or video format.

D Visit the Museum of Broadcast Communications at 360 North State Street. Enjoy some of the thousands of hours of archived television and radio programs available; then write an article about some "hidden treasure" you have discovered.

Decide

A Who is the funniest comic actor or comedian you know? Why do you consider this person to be so funny? Using specific details from this person's body of work, write a persuasive essay using the following thesis starter: "———— is an extremely funny performer because…"

B Featuring such long-running programs as *Bozo's Circus; Garfield Goose and Friend;* and *Kukla, Fran and Ollie,* the late 1940s to the mid-1970s has been described as a "golden age" in Chicago children's television. Would these shows still be popular today, or have they become dated? Watch some vintage episodes of early Chicago children's television. Then write an essay which argues either for or against the timeless appeal of these programs.

Imagine

Write a proposal for an original TV program for kids. Make it an adventure series. The proposal should be short but complete. You are writing this to sell the idea to a big-time TV producer. Choose one of these as a key character in your story:

1 Bilingual raccoon 2 Absent-minded mule 3 Ten-year-old inventor 4 King of Patagonia's servant 5 Abandoned pony 6 Generous old man 7 Martian planning a trip to Earth 8 Seven-year-old explorer 9 Indecisive giant 10 Someone else you can imagine

SEPTEMBER 5, 1964
BEATLES PLAY COMISKEY PARK

The Beatles at Comiskey Park. Negative no. 64847. Photograph by Lenahan for Chicago Daily News, Inc. Chicago History Museum. Image cropped and brightened.

Background

Nothing like this had ever happened in Chicago. On September 5,1964, the Beatles—the immensely popular, sometimes controversial, long-haired, rock-music sensations from Great Britain—put on two performances before wildly enthusiastic crowds at Comiskey Park. This was one of many stops on the Beatles' world tour. The noise from the crowd—made up mostly of young people—was so loud that many said they could not even hear the singers.

Go online to see video footage of the concert.

Check out the archived material on the Beatles at the Museum of Broadcast Communications at 360 North State Street.

Now write a concise summary of what you observed.

Remember

In the 1960s, the Beatles were a huge part of youth culture both in Chicago and throughout America. These days young people may no longer have "Beatlemania," but they do follow other fads common to people all over. What are some of today's fads in…

1 Clothing? 2 Music? 3 Food? 4 Communication? 5 TV shows? 6 Verbal expressions? 7 Celebrity gossip? 8 Movies? 9 Hobbies? 10 Dancing?

Recall a time from your recent past in which you rejected one of these fads. Write a short, personal narrative explaining that episode.

Go Online

Go to **chicago.writethroughamerica.com/beatles** to access useful links and student writing samples for the Discover and Decide prompts.

Discover

A The Beatles phenomenon prompted American teenagers, including many in Chicago and the suburbs, to form their own rock bands. Find out more about local teen bands in the 1960s, and write a newspaper article summarizing what you have discovered about the Chicago garage band scene.

B Chicago radio has a rich Beatles heritage. Local Chicago disc jockey Jim Stagg of radio station WCFL covered the Beatles on three of their U.S. tours, including their visits to Chicago. Dick Biondi has been credited with playing the first Beatles record on American radio when he played "Please Please Me" on WLS in 1963. Create a PowerPoint presentation on Chicago radio in the 1960s.

C The first time many Americans, Chicagoans included, had an opportunity to see the Beatles was on Sunday night television when the band performed on *The Ed Sullivan Show* on February 9, 1964. Go online to watch their performance. Then write a monologue in which a teenage Beatles fan calls his or her best friend to rave about the show.

D Interview older people from Chicago. Do they remember where they were that night in 1964? What other performances can they remember? What kind of music did they enjoy? Accessing the Silver Dollar Survey for September 5, 1964, may help stir up some musical memories.

Decide

A When the Beatles first started producing records, many critics, including many from Chicago, felt that they were just one more passing fad. Examine the Beatles phenomenon and write an essay supporting the thesis: "The Beatles do/do not deserve their legendary status because…"

B In a press conference held in Chicago about a year after the Comiskey Park concert, John Lennon attempted to clarify controversial remarks he had made that threatened to seriously damage the Beatles' following in America. Discover more about the controversy by reading a transcript of the interview and a retrospective on the event.

Then write an essay using the following thesis starter: "Celebrities should/ should not use their status to comment on social issues because…"

Imagine

Imagine that you are a high school sophomore on assignment to cover the concert for your school newspaper. You are invited to attend a press conference after the concert where you can ask one question.

1 With 10 minutes to go before the concert, you take a seat. From where you are sitting, where is the stage? What else can you see?
2 What can't you see?   **3** What does the girl in front of you shout hysterically when the Beatles come on stage?   **4** A grumpy man on the other side of you is complaining. What exactly does he say?
5 A souvenir man comes by. He tries to sell you a Beatles wig. What do you do? What else is he selling?   **6** Police officers are everywhere. Are they prepared to stop a riot? How are they reacting to the singing?
7 What are you doing during all of this?   **8** What was the most exciting moment? The most disappointing? Most surprising?   **9** On the way to the press conference, you hear two people arguing about the Beatles. What are they saying?   **10** At the press conference, you ask one question to the Beatles. What do you ask? What do they answer?

Write a first-person account for your school newspaper. You want the people who read this to understand what it was like being at the performance. Explain what you were hoping to see and what you actually did see. Include lots of details.

JANUARY 26, 1967
RECORD SNOWFALL HITS CHICAGO!

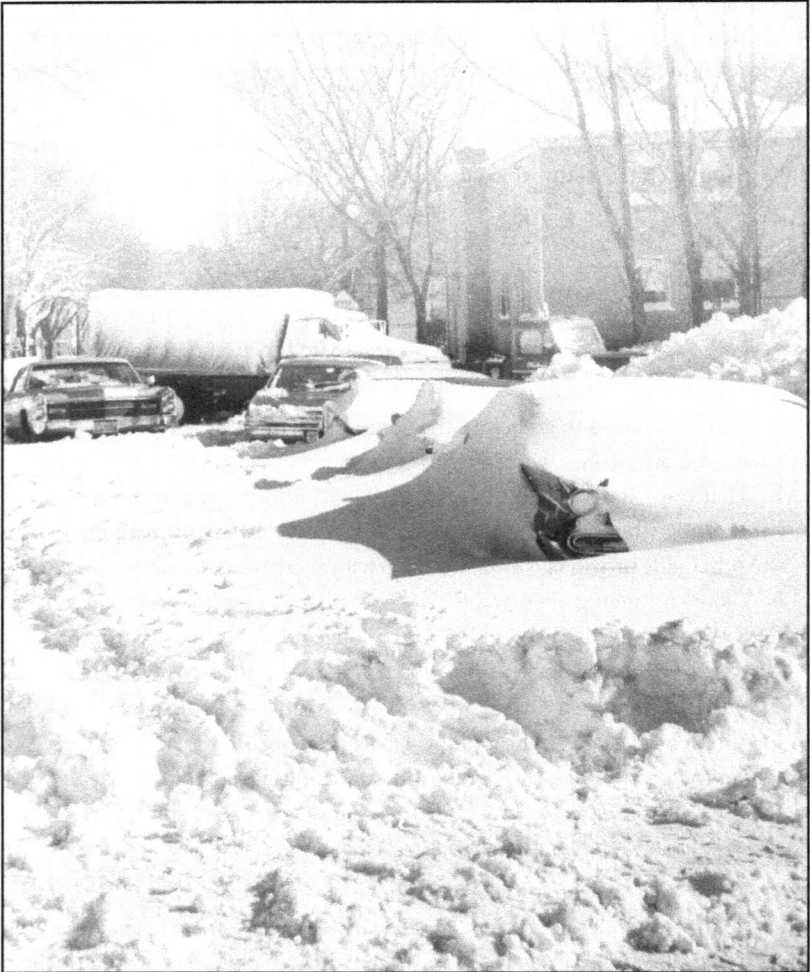

Blizzard of 1967. Photo by Howard B. Anderson. Chicago History Museum. Image cropped.

Background

At 5:02 a.m., on January 26, 1967, the snow started falling. When it stopped at 10:10 a.m. the following day, 23 inches of snow had fallen on the Chicago region. The blizzard claimed 60 lives. Thousands of commuters were stranded, and twenty thousand abandoned cars and 700 CTA buses clogged the streets.

Check out the display devoted to *Science Storms* at the Museum of Science and Industry.

Search the *Chicago Tribune* archives online for articles on the Chicago Blizzard of 1967.

Now that you have familiarized yourself with the events of the Chicago Blizzard of 1967, write a concise summary of the facts of that memorable day.

Remember

Weather matters a lot. Sometimes we can ignore it, but often we cannot and should not. Recall several times when the weather has had an effect on your life. Here are some possible situations:

1 Vacation   2 School   3 Sporting event   4 Camping or other outdoor activity   5 Exercise   6 Work   7 Family matters   8 Hobby   9 Hike   10 Art Project

Write a day-in-the-life account of a time when something you had planned was dramatically affected by the weather—perhaps even in a funny way.

Go Online

Go to **chicago.writethroughamerica.com/blizzard** to access useful links and student writing samples for the Discover and Decide prompts.

Discover

A Chicago has long been known for its severe winter weather. Using data found online, create a bar graph comparing the heaviest snowfalls in Chicago history.

B According to the established criteria of the Northeast Snowfall Impact Scale, the blizzard of 1967 was so severe that it is rated as one of the 10 worst snowstorms in recorded history. Create a PowerPoint presentation or a video about the most devastating snowstorms in history. Consider adding music to enliven your presentation.

C Although Chicago social activist and writer Richard Wright was better known for his prose, he was also a gifted writer of haiku. Many of his poems captured images of winter. Learn more about Wright's poetry; then try your hand at writing some winter haiku of your own.

D Interview some friends or classmates to learn how they would spend an unexpected day off from school. Then write a short essay describing the perfect snow day.

Decide

A Twelve years after the 1967 blizzard, another massive snowfall hit Chicago. The city's administration's inability to deal effectively with the situation led to the defeat of incumbent mayor Michael Bilandic in the 1979 Democratic mayoral primary. Do some research online about the Blizzard of 1979. Then write an essay using this thesis starter: "Michael Bilandic was fairly/unfairly blamed for his role in the Blizzard of 1979 fiasco because…"

B Although many people try to flee the Chicago winters, most people find ways to endure them. Write an editorial arguing that Chicago is a worthwhile place to spend the winter.

Imagine

You lived through the giant snowstorm, but your life was changed in a significant way. You now have a new...

1 Friend.   2 Philosophy of life.   3 Value.   4 Habit.   5 Job.
6 Feeling about yourself.   7 Political opinion.   8 Interest in nature.
9 Attitude toward your home.   10 Attitude toward power.

Choose one, and tell this story to someone who does not believe it's possible for people to really change.

AUGUST 15, 1967
PICASSO SCULPTURE UNVEILED

Pablo Picasso's untitled sculpture. Photograph by Carol M. Highsmith (Library of Congress). Available from loc.gov/pictures/item/2011636144, accessed August 25, 2013.

Background

When Mayor Richard J. Daley pulled the string on August 15, 1967, to unveil the untitled 50-foot, cubist structure, people weren't sure what to think. Afterward, people wondered just what the statue was supposed to be depicting. Although the "Chicago Picasso" has become one of the city's most famous landmarks, Chicagoans still like to share their opinions on this enigmatic work of art.

Check out the Picasso sculpture for yourself at Daley Plaza.

Search online at the Encyclopedia of Chicago on the Chicago History Museum's website to discover more photos, articles, and facts about this controversial piece of art.

Now that you have familiarized yourself with the Picasso sculpture, write a concise summary of the events surrounding the unveiling of this piece of art.

Remember

We've all been in situations in which we've had to explain why we liked something that others did not. Recall a time that you stood up for a film or television program that others didn't like as much as you did.

1 What was the film or program? Why was it supposed to be so good? 2 What did you especially like about the film or program? 3 What did your friends dislike about the film or program? 4 What were your reasons for considering your friends to be wrong? 5 Why did they think you were wrong? 6 Can you repeat dialogue from a few typical argumentative moments? 7 How was the argument resolved? Did anyone change his or her mind? 8 Did this change how you watched movies or programs after this disagreement? 9 When you look back, do you have any regrets? 10 How have your movie or program tastes changed through the years?

Write this as a first-person account. Start the story in the movie theatre or your family room. Use lots of dialogue. Add enough details so that we can imagine what's going on.

Go Online

Go to **chicago.writethroughamerica.com/picasso** to access useful links and student writing samples for the Discover and Decide prompts.

Discover

A Learn more about Pablo Picasso, the man behind the sculpture. Prepare and present a biographical speech on this artist whose sculpture graces Daley Plaza.

B The "Chicago Picasso," while famous, is only one of many public sculptures adorning the city of Chicago. Take your camera and visit a number of these works; then create a PowerPoint presentation or video on public art in Chicago.

C Research the early controversy behind the Picasso sculpture. Make a list of five positive comments and five negative comments made by Chicagoans at the time. Then incorporate a number of these comments into a one-act play or a scene for a movie that takes place at the unveiling of the statue.

D Is taste in art subjective, or is there such a thing as "good taste?" Interview a spectrum of people you know and compare their responses.

Decide

A Although various theories abound, Picasso himself never provided an explanation as to what he was attempting to depict with the famed sculpture. Write a brief essay establishing what you think Picasso was trying to accomplish with this piece of art.

B If you were giving a tour of Chicago to out-of-town friends and only had time to visit one public artwork, would you take them to the Picasso sculpture at Daley Plaza, to *Cloud Gate* ("The Bean") at Millennium Park, or to some other outdoor work? Write an essay defending your choice. Be sure to include quotes on the subject from Chicagoans you know.

Imagine

You are a newspaper reporter covering the unveiling of the Picasso sculpture. Your article will appear in tomorrow's paper. Make up a quote from each of the following people in the crowd:

1 Police officer 2 Emergency-room nurse 3 High-school freshman
4 Artist 5 Politician 6 Model 7 Street musician 8 Cabdriver
9 Housewife 10 College student majoring in art history

Now write the article, incorporating several of the quotes.

OCTOBER 3, 1967
RIVERVIEW PARK CLOSES

Photo of the Whip ride at Riverview Park, Chicago, June 1957. Chicago Photographers-Photographic Illustrations, East Huron Street, Chicago. Available from Wikimedia Commons file: The_Whip_Riverview_Park_Chicago_1957.jpg, accessed August 25, 2013.

Background

Riverview Amusement Park, located along the Chicago River at Western and Belmont Avenues, was a true Chicago institution for generations. With its 120 rides, including six Ferris wheels and a parachute drop, Riverview was truly a place to "laugh your troubles away"—a place to create memories. After 63 years of operation, the park closed on October 3, 1967.

Check out the display devoted to Riverview Park at the *Chicago: Crossroads of America* exhibit at the Chicago History Museum.

Search online at the Encyclopedia of Chicago on the Chicago History Museum's website or visit the Chicago History Museum Store to discover more about Riverview.

Now that you have familiarized yourself with the subject, write a concise summary of the history of Riverview Park.

Remember

What do people remember about Riverview? Ask older people to describe a moment or a scene that captures their memories of Riverview. Talk to your relatives, your neighbors, your teachers, or anyone else who might have rich memories of this place. What do they recall about…

1 The first views of Riverview?   2 Buying tickets?   3 People who worked there?   4 The crowd?   5 Scary stuff?   6 Not so scary stuff? 7 Noise?   8 Smells?   9 Sounds?   10 Food?

Blend these memories into a description entitled "My Riverview."

Go Online

Go to **chicago.writethroughamerica.com/riverview** to access useful links and student writing samples for the Discover, Decide and Imagine prompts.

Discover

A Chicago is claimed as the birthplace of the foot-long hot dog, which supposedly made its debut at Riverview in the 1930s as an inexpensive yet satisfying meal for park patrons. Learn more about the Chicago hot dog and write a report on the history of this popular treat.

B Chicago is the birthplace of both the amusement park midway and the Ferris wheel. Design and share a PowerPoint presentation on the history of amusement parks.

C What type of ride would your perfect amusement park include? Design the ride, including drawings and a description of its operation.

D Would you like to work at an amusement park? You may enjoy checking out the 2009 film *Adventureland* (R), a comedy-drama inspired by director and writer Greg Mottola's own experiences working at an amusement park in the 1980s. Then make a list of reasons why you would or would not consider taking a summer job in an amusement park.

Decide

A For generations of Chicagoans, Riverview was a magical place. Research and read about the history of Riverview. Next design a small museum to commemorate the 63-year history of the park. Consider incorporating various media sources and interactive displays to really bring the park alive for visitors. Write an essay promoting the virtues of your plan.

B Many defunct Chicago institutions are gone and forgotten, but Chicagoans' memories of Riverview remain vivid. Write an essay arguing why you think this particular institution's legacy has been so long lasting.

Imagine

Today you learn that Riverview will be closing its gates after 63 years. You and your "steady" decide to have one last date night at Riverview before it's gone for good.

1 What's your name? How old are you? Where do you go to school?
2 What are you wearing? What is your date wearing?   3 At the last minute, some friends decide to join you. Who are they?   4 What's the first thing you decide to do as you enter the park?   5 After awhile you get hungry. What do you get from the concession stand?   6 What funny thing happens while you are waiting in line to ride the Flying Turns?   7 Your friends get into a shouting match with another couple at the Water Bug bumper boats. What are they so upset about?
8 Name three sounds and three smells that make you think of River-view.   9 What's the last thing you do before you leave the park?
10 Will there be a next date?

Read the short story "The End of Something" by Oak Park native Ernest Hemingway. Then, using the imminent closing of Riverview as the setting, write a short story about a high school couple who must decide if their summer romance will survive the coming of fall.

AUGUST 28, 1968
POLICE CLASH WITH ANTI-WAR DEMONSTRATORS!

Students gathered during the 1968 Democratic National Convention. Photo by Peter Bullock. Chicago History Museum. Image cropped.

Background

In August of 1968, thousands of delegates to the Democratic National Convention poured into Chicago to select the next Democratic candidate for president. They were joined by thousands of demonstrators. Most of these demonstrators were protesting the war in Vietnam, but others seized the opportunity to express their views about war in general, racism, sexism, and other others issues that were dividing the country. Also in Chicago that week in August, to keep the peace, were hundreds of police officers and soldiers from the National Guard. On August 28, 1968, the volatile mixture of demonstrators and massed police officers exploded.

Check out the display devoted to the 1968 Democratic National Convention at the *Chicago: Crossroads of America* exhibit at the Chicago History Museum.

Search online at the Encyclopedia of Chicago at the Chicago History Museum's website to discover more photos, articles, and facts about this turbulent year in Chicago history.

Write a concise summary of the events of August 28, 1968, in Chicago.

Remember

Chicago in the summer of 1968 was a noisy, chaotic, opinionated place. People did not hold back in expressing their feelings about the war and other issues of the time. Today people get just as excited about national and international topics, such as...

1 Environmental issues.   2 Public education.   3 Immigration.
4 U.S. military involvement.   5 Censorship of books.   6 Gun control.   7 Same-sex marriage.   8 Decriminalization of marijuana.
9 College and professional sports.   10 Political correctness.

As you see it, which one of these issues is debated most heatedly? Write an explanation of this issue and summarize the various positions people can take.

Go Online

Go to **chicago.writethroughamerica.com/convention** to access useful links and student writing samples for the Discover and Decide prompts.

Discover

A Abbie Hoffman, founder of the Youth International Party (Yippies), was arrested for conspiring to disrupt the convention and crossing state lines with the intent to riot as a result of his involvement in the protests in Chicago. Research the life of this controversial political and social activist and create a timeline of significant events in his career.

B How much does the Occupy Chicago movement of 2012 resemble the Yippie movement of 1968? Create a poster comparing and contrasting the two movements and use the poster as a visual aid when you give a short speech on the subject to your class.

C In 2018 the city of Chicago will have to determine how best to acknowledge the 50th anniversary of the 1968 Democratic National Convention. Design an appropriate commemorative plaque and decide where in the city it should be displayed.

D Interview people who have strong memories of the 1968 Convention. What do they remember most? Looking at some photos online may help stir their memories and give you some insights. Write an article and illustrate it with a few of the photos you've examined.

Decide

A Go online to watch the PBS film *Chicago 10*. Observe how director Brett Morgen mixes animation with archival footage to convey the atmosphere before, during, and after this explosive week in the history of both Chicago and the nation. Then write a one-page review arguing whether or not Morgen's treatment of the events is biased in its perspective.

B The rock band Crosby, Stills, Nash &, and Young recorded and performed Graham Nash's song "Chicago" to protest the events that transpired at the 1968 Democratic National Convention. Should musicians use their celebrity status to influence others' views? Research the history of protest music. Then write an essay using the following thesis starter to argue your position: "It is appropriate/inappropriate for celebrities to use their status to influence political beliefs because…"

Imagine

Imagine that in 1968 you are a college student from a nearby small town. You have come to Chicago not as a delegate or as a protestor, but instead because you like to be where the action is. You are naturally curious. You attend demonstrations outside and hang around the convention. You talk with dozens of people and write down quotes. What does each of the people below say to you? Limit each quote to a sentence or two.

1 Police officer who wrestles a demonstrator into a paddy wagon
2 Bleeding demonstrator   3 Mayor's chief of staff   4 Young National Guardsman   5 Argumentative antiwar professor   6 Street minister   7 Delegate from Iowa   8 Pacifist   9 Mother whose son was killed in Vietnam   10 Angry feminist

Back home, you write a letter to a friend. You want this person to understand what you learned from your visit to Chicago and from the people you met. Incorporate the quotes you collected. Explain what you believed before the convention and then what you learned about current events and human nature during your time in Chicago.

JANUARY 1, 1971
BIOGRAPHY OF MAYOR STIRS CONTROVERSY

Chicago Mayor Richard J. Daley. Photo by Chicago Daily News, Inc. Chicago History Museum. Image cropped and brightened.

Background

In 1971, Mike Royko, one of Chicago's most widely read columnists, published an unauthorized biography of Mayor Richard J. Daley. The book, titled *Boss*, was a best seller but was not so popular with the Daley people, who thought it was far too critical of the mayor.

Royko, who wrote a daily political column, was known for his humor and uncompromising stands against power figures. He won a Pulitzer Prize and many other awards for his writing.

Check out the Mike Royko Papers in the Roger and Julie Baskes Department of Special Collecions at the Newberry Library at 60 West Walton Street.

Search online at the Encyclopedia of Chicago on the Chicago History Museum's website to discover more articles and facts about this outspoken newsman.

Now write a concise summary of Royko's journalistic career.

Remember

Even people who disagreed with Royko's politics enjoyed his humorous anecdotes about Chicago. Often these stories described ceremonies or events that did not work out as planned. Write a funny true story about a ceremony that you were part of that failed.

1 How old were you? What were you like at that age? 2 What was the event? 3 What was supposed to happen? 4 Were you a participant in the event or a spectator? 5 When did things start going badly? 6 When were you sure the event was definitely going to fail? 7 What happened immediately afterward? 8 What were the long-term consequences? 9 Did this remind you of anything else? 10 What did you learn?

Write this in a first-person, present-tense form. Give an eyewitness version of what happened.

Go Online

Go to **chicago.writethroughamerica.com/mroyko** to access useful links and student writing samples for the Discover and Decide prompts.

Discover

A One of the most memorable reactions to the unveiling of the "Chicago Picasso" sculpture came from Mike Royko: "Interesting design, I'm sure. But the fact is, it has a long stupid face and looks like some giant insect that is about to eat a smaller, weaker insect." Research Royko's career and jot down some of his other memorable lines.

B Mimicking Royko's blunt sense of humor, write an article that satirizes an issue affecting your school or community.

C Select your favorite from the list of Royko quotes you have compiled. Design either a poster or a T-shirt to illustrate it.

D Visit the Newberry Library and examine its collection of the "works, articles, columns, drafts, research and subject material, correspondence, personal items, mementoes, awards, and photographs reflecting the life and career of Mike Royko." Write an article examining some aspect of Royko's professional or personal life that you find interesting.

Decide

A Is there still a role for newspapers in the 21st century, or should they be completely replaced by digital media? Research the issue and write an essay arguing your position on the matter. Be sure to include quotes from people you know on both sides of the question.

B Between Richard J. Daley and his son Richard M. Daley, the office of mayor was held by someone named Daley for 42 years. Which one of the two Daleys, however, left the stronger legacy? As a small group project, research the careers of the two Mayor Daleys and conduct a debate addressing the question: "Which Mayor Daley left the most lasting impression on the city of Chicago?"

Imagine

Mayor Richard J. Daley had great political strength. He was definitely in charge. Royko was critical of how he gained his power and how he used it, but Daley remained in office until he died. What, in your view, makes a good leader? Must this person be...

1 Intelligent? 2 Articulate? 3 Popular? 4 Well-connected?
5 Fearless? 6 Perceptive? 7 Cunning? 8 Cautious?
9 Forgiving? 10 Creative?

Pick the one descriptive word that you consider to be the most necessary for being an effective leader. Create several short anecdotes to illustrate your point, presenting them as if you will use them to sway someone who has a different point of view.

1974
STUDS TERKEL PUBLISHES WORKING

Studs Terkel. Photograph by James Warden. Available from Wikimedia Commons file: Studs Turkel.jpg, accessed August 20, 2013.

Background

If you read the works of Studs Terkel, you're going to learn a lot about Chicago people. Studs talked to all kinds of people from Chicago, wrote down what they said, and put their words into books. One of his most popular books was *Working,* in which real people, most of them from Chicago, talked about their jobs. It became a best seller and was eventually made into a musical.

Check out the Studs Terkel/WFMT Oral History Archives at the Chicago History Museum.

Search online at the Encyclopedia of Chicago on the Chicago History Museum's website to discover more about the career of this writer and Chicago activist.

Now write a concise summary of Studs Terkel's career.

Remember

What experiences have you had that would qualify or disqualify you from these jobs? Be brief and specific.

1 Police officer   2 Lawyer   3 Kindergarten teacher   4 Spy
5 Taxidermist   6 Social worker   7 Travel agent   8 Clown
9 Politician   10 Pilot

Select one for which you are *not* qualified. Expand your answer by revealing some incidents from your past.

Go Online

Go to **chicago.writethroughamerica.com/sterkel** to access useful links and student writing samples for the Discover and Decide prompts.

Discover

A Pick an occupation that you find intriguing, and learn more about its requirements and responsibilities. Then write a one-page report about what you have discovered.

B Individually or as a small-group project, interview a number of working people from your school or beyond and compile their stories into a series of monologues. Then deliver the monologues "in character" to the class.

C Visit the Chicago History Museum and take the *In Our Own Words* audio tour. Inspired by the museum's Studs Terkel collection, this audio features Chicago teens' interpretations of seven of the museum's *Chicago: Crossroads of America* galleries. If you prefer, you can make a "visit" by downloading the audio tour to an MP3 player. Afterward, write a new segment for the tour based on one of the other *Crossroads* displays.

D The Studs Terkel Community Media Awards are presented annually by the Community Media Workshop at Columbia College to honor "outstanding media professionals for excellence in covering and reflecting Chicago's diverse communities." Go to the Community Media Workshop's website to read from the work of past award winners, and write a tribute article on one of the journalists whose work you admire.

Decide

A How would you define a "successful" career? Salary? Security? Service? Satisfaction? Write an essay in which you outline your criteria for success.

B What if your school offered a work-study program in which a semester's credit could be earned by working at a job outside of the classroom, if the job provided both a worthwhile learning experience for you and a service to the community? Write a proposal to your school's administration describing your choice of job and explaining how it meets these two requirements.

Imagine

Imagine your dream job. It's something you would enjoy and would do well. It would pay you enough to live comfortably. It would provide the challenges and variety to keep you developing as a person. Pretend that someone like Studs Terkel is interviewing you about this perfect job.

1 What is the job? Be specific.   2 How much education and training are necessary for you to get hired?   3 What unique skills do you bring to the job?   4 What are some of your daily duties and responsibilities? 5 What are some of the job's biggest challenges?   6 What would be a bad day?   7 What would be a good day?   8 How would you grow as a person because of this job?   9 What does your work contribute to society?   10 How do you see the job changing as you approach retirement?

Present this in a question/answer format.

JULY 12, 1979
RIOT AT COMISKEY PARK!

Outside of Old Comiskey Park. Photograph by Johnmaxmena2. Available from Wikimedia Commons file: Oldcomiskeypark1986a.jpg, accessed August 25, 2013.

Background

As the decade of the 1970s drew to a close, radio station WLUP-FM and the Chicago White Sox teamed up on a promotion to draw more fans to a double-header on the night of July 12, 1979. The event, called Disco Demolition Night, offered a 98¢ admission to any fan who brought along a disco record to be ceremoniously "demolished" by a popular local disc jockey named Steve Dahl. Although the promoters were anticipating a crowd of perhaps 12,000 people, 60,000 arrived. Matters quickly got out of control, and thousands stormed the field between games, resulting in enough arrests, injuries, and general destruction to force the White Sox to forfeit the second game to the Detroit Tigers.

Visit the National Radio Hall of Fame at the Museum of Broadcast Communications at 360 North State Street in Chicago to learn more about one of its 2013 inductees, Steve Dahl, the man behind Disco Demolition Night.

Go online to the *Chicago Tribune* archives to read articles about Disco Demolition Night.

Now write a concise summary of what you have discovered about Disco Demolition Night at the old Comiskey Park.

Remember

Few of us could claim that we ever had an idea with as many unintended consequences as Disco Demolition, but we all have had bad ideas. We thought something was going to work a certain way, but it didn't. Often, we set out to solve one problem and in the process created many other problems. Pick one of your own doozies and share the experience.

1 How old were you at the time? What were your main interests?
2 What was the problem you wanted to solve? 3 What solutions were you considering? 4 Why did you come up with this idea?
5 How did you imagine that things would work out if all went well?
6 What was the first indication that the plan might not be so good?
7 What did you do when things started to fall apart? 8 How did the experience end? 9 What were some of the immediate consequences?
10 When you look back now, what strikes you as especially significant about the event?

Retell this as a cautionary tale. Explain, if you can, the fatal mistake.

Go Online

Go to **chicago.writethroughamerica.com/discoriot** to access useful links and student writing samples for the Discover and Decide prompts.

Discover

A Although legendary Chicago sports broadcaster Harry Caray (then-White Sox announcer) would not have considered Disco Demolition Night as a high point in his career, there were plenty of other events along the way to make up for it. Learn more about Harry Caray's career, and write a one-page tribute to this Chicago sports icon.

B Violence among sports fans is not just a recent issue. In 532 A.D., friction between supporters of the rival Blue and Green chariot racing teams in Constantinople (now Istanbul) resulted in widespread destruction and the deaths of tens of thousands of people. Create a PowerPoint presentation on the Nika riots.

C Disco Demolition Night was not the only baseball promotion that did not turn out as expected. Investigate the history of some of the worst ideas in sports promotion. Then design a series of your own "terrible" promotions, complete with posters advertising the upcoming events.

D The anti-disco movement has been branded by some as racist and homophobic. Others deny that accusation and argue that the movement was motivated by strong musical preferences. Research the controversy and write an essay defending or attacking the anti-disco movement.

Decide

A Few, if any, ballpark promotions have ever turned out as disastrously as Disco Demolition Night. Make a list of 10 factors that contributed to its failure, and rank them from least to most responsible for the debacle. Briefly justify your rankings.

B Although Disco Demolition Night was the brainchild of his son, Michael, flamboyant White Sox owner Bill Veeck was well known for his own wacky promotions and gimmicks, including his most famous publicity stunt in which 3' 7" Eddie Gaedel pinch hit for the 1951 St. Louis Browns. Although Veeck always denied it, many believe the stunt was inspired by James Thurber's short story, "You Could Look it Up." Read the story and decide for yourself. Explain why you have come to this conclusion.

Imagine

It's 1979, and you are a journalism major at DePaul University working as a student intern for the *Chicago Tribune*. When you are asked to write a short article on Disco Demolition Night, you think it will be a routine assignment. However, you are in for a big surprise. What do these people say to you about the night's events?

1 Broadcaster 2 White Sox player 3 Detroit Tiger coach 4 Serious baseball fan 5 White Sox batboy 6 Security guard 7 College student/disco hater 8 Hot dog vendor 9 High-school sophomore/disco lover 10 Baseball historian

Make up the eyewitness reaction of each of these people in 20 or fewer words.

JANUARY 26, 1986
CHICAGO BEARS WIN SUPER BOWL XX!

Art Institute of Chicago lions celebrate the Bears. Photograph by Chris Diers. Available from Wikimedia Commons file: Lion_Chicago_Bears_Helmet_.jpg, accessed August 20, 2013.

Background

It had been more than 20 years since the Chicago Bears, once one of the most feared teams in the National Football League, had been champions. And some of those years had been truly awful. The 1969 team, for example, won only one game. But since the early 1980s the team had been getting better every year. They had a savvy general manager, a colorful coach, and great players, four of whom became Hall of Famers.

In the 1985 season their record was 15-1. They roared through the playoffs. On January 26, 1986, they played the New England Patriots in a Super Bowl held in New Orleans and won 46-10.

Check out the display devoted to the Chicago Bears at the *Chicago: Crossroads of America* exhibit at the Chicago History Museum.

Search online at the Chicagoland Sports Hall of Fame website to discover more photos, articles, and facts about Chicago's NFL team.

Now write a concise summary of the Chicago Bears' championship season of 1985.

Remember

Recall a time that you were part of a successful team or school group. People had different roles on this team or with this group, and they played them well.

1 How old were you at the time?   2 What was the group?   3 Why were you in it?   4 What was your role?   5 What were other roles?
6 What did you have to accomplish?   7 How did things begin?
8 What challenges did you face?   9 How did your group finally succeed?   10 How do you feel about it now?

Write this as a folktale. Begin with "Once upon a time…"

Go Online

Go to **chicago.writethroughamerica.com/superbowl** to access useful links and student writing samples for the Discover and Decide prompts.

Discover

A In the years before the first Super Bowl, the NFL Championship game was played to determine the best team in professional football. The most convincing victory in NFL history was the 1940 Championship game in which the Chicago Bears defeated the Washington Redskins by the almost-unbelievable score of 73-0. Research this remarkable game, and write a retrospective article on the contest.

B Prior to their Super Bowl victory, the Chicago Bears' "Shufflin' Crew" recorded "The Super Bowl Shuffle," a rap song that went on to sell a half-million copies and receive a Grammy nomination for rhythm and blues performance by a duo or group. Go online and watch the Shufflin' Crew's video for inspiration. Then write your own rap dedicated to a team, club, or organization of your own choosing. As a small group project, choreograph and perform your rap for your class.

C A phenomenon has developed that involves the ads that run during the Super Bowl broadcast. It has reached a point that many people tune in to watch the Super Bowl not for the game itself but instead to catch the commercials. In 2013, thirty seconds of airplay cost 3.5 million dollars or more. With such astronomical prices, advertisers look to make their commercials as memorable as they can. Pick a product and write a script for your own Super Bowl commercial. Don't be afraid to make it outlandish!

D Ever since the rival Chicago Cardinals moved to St. Louis in 1960, the Chicago Bears have been the only NFL team in town. Interview diehard Bears fans of various ages about their favorite memories of "Da Bears," and compile their reflections into a PowerPoint presentation accompanied by some vintage pictures.

Decide

A Recent concerns over player safety in football, especially regarding the long-term effects of concussions, have led to new rule changes designed to cut down on injuries. Some football fans argue, however, that these changes will eventually detract from the game's popularity. Research the controversy and form your own opinion on the issue. Then write an essay to offer your viewpoint about how extensive the rule changes should be.

B Although some might disagree, many sports historians rank the 1985 Chicago Bears as the greatest NFL team of all time. Research the other great teams in NFL history that might lay claim to this title, and write an article supporting your choice.

Imagine

Many of the '85 Bears had colorful nicknames. The quarterback was "The Punky QB." A linebacker called himself "Mama's Boy Otis." Other players had names like "The Refrigerator," "Danimal," "Mongo," and "Sweetness." Coach Ditka was known as "Iron Mike."

Here are ten made-up nicknames:

1 "Flaky Phil" **2** "The Wanderer" **3** "Noodles" **4** "Next time Nelly" **5** "The Cave Man" **6** "Volcano Vic" **7** "Stone Hands" **8** "Feathers" **9** "Smoke Brain" **10** "Lightning Legs"

Write character sketches for five of the "athletes" above. The sketch should explain the nickname.

JUNE 14, 1998
BULLS REPEAT THREE-PEAT

Chicago Bulls basketball game. Photograph by Carol M. Highsmith. Carol M. Highsmith Archive
(Library of Congress). Available from loc.gov/pcitures/item/2011635549, accessed August 25, 2013.

Background

There had been many great sports teams in Chicago, but never a dynasty—
no team had won over and over and over again. At least, no team had done so
until the Bulls in the 1990s. Crowds packed the United Center (and its pre-
decessor, the Chicago Stadium) to watch the city's extraordinary professional
basketball team. During the playoffs, restaurant business was down in Chicago because so many Chicagoans were staying home to watch their team on TV.
For Chicago sports fans, who through the years had often been let down by
the home teams, it was truly a special time. On June 14, 1998, the Bulls won
their sixth NBA title in eight years, taking three in a row twice, from 1991 to
1993 and 1996 to 1998.

Michael Jordan had much to do with this. Few athletes have played so con-
sistently well, especially during crucial games. Most writers and basketball in-
siders agree that MJ was the best player ever.

Search the *Chicago Tribune* archives online for articles on the Chicago
Bulls' six championship seasons.

Search online at the Chicagoland Sports Hall of Fame website to discover more photos, articles, and facts about Chicago's NBA team.

Now write a concise summary of the Bulls' success in the 1990s.

Remember

Consider your own sports history —good, bad, or otherwise—and come up
with a memory that fits one of the following headlines:

1 *I Finally Did It!*   2 *Almost.*   3 *What Luck!*   4 *What Was I Thinking?*   5 *A Team Effort.*   6 *A Tough Way to Learn a Lesson.*   7 *We
Just Weren't Ready.*   8 *Practice Paid Plenty.*   9 *What a Teammate!*
10 *I Think I'll Try Another Sport.*

Write this up as a personal narrative. Include your feelings and reactions.

Go Online

Go to **chicago.writethroughamerica.com/threepeat** to access useful links and student writing samples for the Discover and Decide prompts.

Discover

A Almost 50 years before the Bulls clinched their second three-peat, Chicago native and DePaul University graduate George Mikan was the best player in professional basketball. The first dominant "big man," the 6' 10" Mikan went on to lead the Minneapolis Lakers to five championships and was named "Best Basketball Player of the First Half of the Twentieth Century" in a poll by the Associated Press. Write an article on Chicago's first "Mr. Basketball."

B Although being a Chicago sports fan can be frustrating at times, in the 1990s Chicago was the center of the basketball world. Using a timeline as a visual aid, give a speech on the "golden age" of Chicago basketball.

C When the Chicago Bulls take the court at the United Center, they run out to the distinctive music of the song "Sirius" by the Alan Parsons Project. Imagine that you have been commissioned to write a poem or rap about the Bulls that would accompany that song. Once finished, try recording the words yourself.

D Anyone who ever saw Michael Jordan play will never forget the magic he brought to the basketball court. Interview friends and relatives who enjoyed Jordan's career, and compile their comments into a tribute article.

Decide

A Baseball has long been called America's national pastime, but is that still the case? Many sports fans argue that either football or basketball is now number one, while others claim that soccer, hockey, or NASCAR racing hold the title. Decide on three criteria or areas by which to judge the popularity of these sports, and then write a persuasive essay establishing which sport is truly America's national pastime.

B The 1995–1996 Chicago Bulls set a record for most wins in the regular season, going 72-10 (a winning percentage of .878) and eventually winning 15 of 18 playoff games on their way to the NBA Championship. Would you agree with those who claim that they were the best team of all time? Research the other great basketball teams in history and write an article supporting your choice.

Imagine

A medium-sized city is debating whether or not to use city funds to expand the downtown basketball arena. This would cost a lot of money, but it will also attract better players and maybe help the local professional team become champions. The mayor calls for a meeting to discuss the question: "Does a championship team help a city?" From the following list of 10 people, choose four as participants. Each will express a different point of view.

1 Head of tourism   2 Social worker   3 Owner of the team
4 Local TV announcer   5 Sociology professor at the city college
6 Cabdriver   7 Cultural director   8 Head of the teachers'
union   9 Police chief   10 Local restaurant owner

You are a local journalist covering the story. Write a short, succinct article summarizing the debate.

NOVEMBER 4, 2008
OBAMA DELIVERS VICTORY SPEECH IN CHICAGO

Barack Obama on Election Night in 2008, Grant Park. Photograph by Gabbec. Available from Wikimedia Commons file: Obama08acceptance.jpg, accessed August 20, 2013.

Background

On the evening of Tuesday, November 4, 2008, Barack Obama held a victory celebration in Grant Park. Many in the crowd of 240,000 spectators were African Americans celebrating the election of the first black president. Around the world, millions more listened to his speech in which, like most victorious candidates through the years, he vowed to work hard to solve the many problems the country faced.

Chicago was the president-elect's adopted hometown. As a young man he had worked in Chicago. He had married a girl from Chicago. He owned a house in Chicago. He was a state senator representing his Chicago neighborhood and later served as a United States senator from Illinois.

Go to the WTTW website to access photos, articles, and documentary footage on the history of Chicago's African American community from the arrival of Jean-Baptiste Pointe DuSable through the presidential election of Barack Obama.

Search online at the Encyclopedia of Chicago on the Chicago History Museum's website to discover more photos, articles, and facts about Barack Obama

---

Now write a concise summary of the election of the 44th president of the United States.

Remember

On the stage that night, along with Vice President-elect Biden and his family, were Barack Obama's wife Michelle and his children Sasha, age seven, and Malia, 10. Both girls were born and raised in Chicago, and now they were about to move to Washington, D.C., to live in the White House. Their father had promised them a dog, a normal enough gift, but nothing would be normal about the life they were about to enter.

Using examples from your own past, explain why or why not you would want to be the child of the president. Before writing, consider how you feel about...

1 Privacy.   2 Bodyguards.   3 Big houses.   4 Photographers.
5 Dressing up.   6 Travel.   7 Gossip.   8 Formal meals.   9 Smiling all the time.   10 Hearing your parents criticized on television.

Go Online

Go to **chicago.writethroughamerica.com/obama** to access useful links and student writing samples for the Discover and Decide prompts.

Discover

A *It winds from Chicago to LA,*
More than two thousand miles all the way.
Get your kicks on Route Sixty-six. (Bobby Troup, "Route 66")

The eastern terminus of the famed Route 66 was actually Grant Park. Go online to listen to Chicagoan Nat King Cole's rendition of the song. Now learn more about the history of Route 66 and write an article about America's fascination with this legendary highway.

B Barack Obama's presidential election adds another chapter to the African American experience in Chicago. Research another significant event, such as the Great Migration from the South, the 1919 Race Riots, Ernie Banks' 500th home run, the election of Harold Washington, or the Oprah Winfrey phenomenon. Give a speech on the subject to your class.

C Write a short children's book about an elderly person who attempts to explain to his or her young grandchild why November 4, 2008, is such a remarkable day in the family's history. Be sure to illustrate the book with your own pictures or clip art.

D Find some of the 240,000 people who attended the election night rally and celebration at Grant Park on November 4, 2008, and interview them about the experience. Then using excerpts from their recollections, design a series of posters commemorating the event.

Decide

A Chicago natives Hillary Clinton and Michelle Obama, the 42nd and 44th First Ladies of the United States, have both been advocates for political and social issues. How important, though, is the role of the wife of the president of the United States? Learn about the evolution of this position, and write an essay outlining the attributes necessary to be an effective first lady.

B If you could go back in time and safely witness one event in Chicago history, which one would it be? Select the moment and write an essay justifying your choice.

Imagine

Pretend that you have just been elected mayor of Chicago. At the victory celebration, you identify 10 areas that concern you. Here's the list in alphabetical order:

1 Crime   2 Economy   3 Libraries   4 Museums   5 Parks
6 Race relations   7 Schools   8 Senior citizens   9 Tourism
10 Transportation

Rearrange these, starting with what you consider to be the most important and ending with the least important. Then explain why you chose a certain area as the most important issue facing the city.

40 MORE PROVOCATIVE CHICAGO HEADLINES

Now that you've had an opportunity to use the *Write Through Chicago* approach to "learn about a city by writing about a city," you may want to do some further research of your own choosing. Here are 40 more Chicago headlines for you to examine and some questions to help you get started:

1 What can you learn about this event from readily available sources? **2** What people would have responded to this headline? **3** Why would this event have mattered to these people? **4** What changes in Chicago, if any, might this event have brought about? **5** How, in any way, can you identify with this event? **6** How could you make this the subject of a piece of creative writing?

1673	Marquette and Joliet Arrive
1837	Ogden Becomes First Mayor
1848	Waterway to the Mississippi Completed
1855	Closing of Bars Leads to Riots
1860	Republicans Nominate Lincoln for President
1872	Montgomery Ward Starts First Mail-Order House
1887	Art Institute Opens
1889	Sullivan and Adler Complete Auditorium Theater
1900	Direction of Chicago River Reversed
1904	Ravinia Park Opens
1905	Chicago Defender Debuts
1905	I.W.W. Starts
1919	Race Riot Spreads Through City
1920	"Hinky Dink" and "Bathhouse John" Rule the Levee
1924	Two University of Chicago Students Commit "Crime of the Century"
1927	Tunney Defeats Dempsey in "Long Count" Prize Fight

1929	New Leader at University of Chicago
1929	Globetrotters Get Started
1930	Swimming Champ to Play Tarzan
1937	115,000 Attend High School Football Game
1939	Saul Alinsky Organizes a Neighborhood
1942	Nuclear Chain Reaction in Hyde Park
1950	Nelson Algren Wins National Book Award
1959	The Second City Theater Opens
1966	Martin Luther King, Jr., Marches Through the City
1966	Killing in Kenilworth
1969	Loyola Captures NCAA Basketball Championship
1970	Northwestern Students Go on Strike
1974	Steppenwolf Theater Company Founded
1977	Nazis Plan to March in Skokie
1978	Milton Friedman Wins Noble Prize
1978	El Derailed in Loop
1981	Spider Man Scales Sears Tower
1983	Chicago Elects First Black Mayor
1984	Chicago Hosts First Poetry Slam
1986	The Oprah Winfrey Show Begins
1987	Mr. T. Cuts Down Trees in Lake Forest
1995	Ferris Wheel at Navy Pier
2004	Millennium Park Completed
2009	Rahm Emanuel Takes Over

Mark Henry Larson

Bob Boone

ABOUT THE AUTHORS

Longtime teachers and writers Mark Henry Larson and Bob Boone have collaborated for more than thirty years. Along with coauthoring *Write Through Chicago,* they have written two other creative writing books, *Moe's Cafe* and *Joan's Junk Shop.* They have taught an online creative writing course for Northwestern University's Center for Talent Development and now manage a website for teachers, **writethroughamerica.com**. Larson and Boone also conduct workshops to help teachers incorporate creative writing into their classrooms. In the future they plan to establish a center for the support of creative writing. On his own, Boone has written a sports biography, a memoir, and a collection of short stories. Larson is the coauthor of the *Creative Writing Handbook* and various articles on writing and teaching.

www.ingramcontent.com/pod-product-compliance
Lightning Source LLC
Chambersburg PA
CBHW052045090426
42739CB00010B/2052